Living Simultaneously

To Chris.

Living Simultaneously

BALANCING SELF-CARE,
PERSONAL RELATIONSHIPS AND WORK

by

Jeffrey Patnaude

You are a channel of our Lord's Light. May you forever embrace your anointing.

WHITE RHINO PRESS
Greensboro, North Carolina

In Christ,
Jeff

January 2012

(}

Living Simultaneously
Copyright 2001 by Jeffrey Patnaude

White Rhino Press
3707-B W. Market Street
Greensboro, NC 27403

Cover design by Cale Burr, Bellevue, WA
Typesetting by Linda Davis — Star Type, Berkeley, CA
Back Cover Photography by L. Leigh Glasgow Photography, Greensboro, NC

Library of Congress Cataloging-in-Publication Data
LCCN 2001 135065

ISBN 0-9704122-0-7

First Edition 2001
Printed in the United States of America

Contents

Acknowledgments

Any creation is a collection of wisdom and experience from travelers on the same path. I thank all who have contributed to this work for without them, it may have been just another idea, on a page of one of many journals. My deepest appreciation to the following people and one incredible friend:

Carol Brown who encouraged me to write this book sooner rather than later; Mary Matthiesen, my vibrant friend and almost first co-author who helped me get started; Emily Wilmer, my long-time friend and almost second co-author who made many contributions in the introduction and elsewhere; Joy Sigmon, my friend and colleague who monitored this production right to the last word; agent Victoria Shoemaker for her kind wisdom and counsel, John O'Donohue for his beautiful gift of *A Blessing*, Marcia Bauman for her thoughtful editing; my daughters Julie and Laura for providing some good material from the substance of their lovely lives; my wife, Mary Margaret for her keen sense about reorganizing the book in a way much better than my original thinking; my two sisters Barbara Barden and Cynthia Patrick for allowing me to include "stuff" from our childhood (I didn't ask permission); my many friends whom I have referred to in the text: Angeles Arrien, William Lewis, Laura Lewis, William Woodward, Ryan Ruch, Emily Gutherie, John Chambers, Beth, Kingsford and Wyatt Jones, Joyce Thompson, Margaret More, Barbie Lussier, Sam and Ulele Hamway, Jim Bronson, Gordon Wells, Carmela Tomasini, my Stanford football buddies, Marvin and Ressa, colleague and on-going support person, Mark Sabin, my first band, Tommy Pratt, Howard Hopkins, Gary Raynor and Billie Madison and my first kiss, Michele Drew.

Finally, my thanks to Bear, the Golden Retriever who snores at my feet, unaware that some day, I want to grow up to be just like him.

A BLESSING

May you listen to your longing to be free.

May the frames of your belonging be large enough
for the dreams of your soul.

May you arise each day with a voice of blessing
whispering in your heart that something good is going
to happen to you.

May you find a harmony between your soul and your life.

May the mansion of your soul never become a haunted place.

May you know the eternal longing which lives
at the heart of time.

May there be kindness in your gaze when you look within.

May you never place walls between the light and yourself.

May your angel free you from the prisons of guilt,
fear, disappointment, and despair.

May you allow the wild beauty of the invisible world to
gather you, mind you, and embrace you in belonging.

JOHN O'DONOHUE
by permission, from "Eternal Echoes"
Harper Collins 1999

Dedication

This book is dedicated to my spiritual friend, the mystical one who lives life with ease, balance, and celebration—our dog Bear.

IF A DOG WERE YOUR TEACHER,
YOU WOULD LEARN THINGS LIKE . . .

- when loved ones come home, always run to greet them.

- never pass up the opportunity to go for a joyride.

- allow the experience of fresh air and the wind
  in your face to be pure ecstasy.

- when it's in your best interest—practice obedience.

- let others know when they've invaded your territory.

- take naps and stretch before rising.

- run, romp, and play daily.

- thrive on attention and let people touch you.

- avoid biting when a simple growl will do.

- on warm days, stop to lie on your back in the grass.

- on hot days, drink lots of water and lie under a shady tree.

- when you're happy, dance around and wag your entire body.

- no matter how often you're scolded, don't buy into the
  guilt thing and pout . . . run right back and make friends.

- delight in the simple joy of a long walk.

- eat with gusto and enthusiasm and stop when
  you have had enough.

- be loyal.

- never pretend to be something you are not.

- if what you want lies buried, dig until you find it.

- when someone is having a bad day, be silent, sit close by,
  and nuzzle them gently.

AUTHOR UNKNOWN

Introduction

The Universe offers each of us an invitation to the bountiful feast
of a life of playfulness, laughter, love, and creativity.
Whether or not we attend the party is a matter of personal choice.

Most of us have operated in such overload for so long that the norm becomes *The Way of Too*—*too* much, *too* fast, *too* often, and perhaps *too* little, *too* late. Writing this book has challenged that particular aspect of my being and called me to change when I discovered that all three of my life circles needed revision. It has not been easy, since such a challenge to change can produce panic, if not crippling fear. Hanging back was my natural inclination but the call to change—for me—was inescapable.

My first action in response to this need to change was to "get organized"—organize every *part* of my life. But that was a problem. Life is not in parts. In fact, if I thought of myself as having separate lives—my "personal life," "my "work life," my "family life," my "love life," my "recreational life," my "spiritual life"—I would fail to discover that these many "lives" are really all *one* life. Thus, I cannot send the mind to work, reserve the heart for the family, or schedule play for my individual self. When I work I create, when I create I play, when I play I love, and when I love I create. I discovered that my life is really one continuous flow. When I live each day in this endless flow, I am *living simultaneously.*

Perhaps your first attempt at achieving the elusive luxury of life-balance is the same action that I took—*compartmentalize:* get better organized, join a gym, take a vacation, create a partner date-night or somehow find more time. By dissecting our lives—examining how we spend our time, repositioning our focus and our energies, we think we have created the perfect formula for balance. But then something happens: the next day arrives and all has changed. So we begin again. Although we try to make life less complicated by dividing it into more manageable parts, we often actually create more complexity instead.

The dominant world-view of Sir Issac Newton and "mechanistic theory," has led us to believe that balance comes from achieving order through compartmentalizing, organizing and prioritizing. Although such characteristics can be a product of a life in balance, this book is not a "how-to" manual for cleaning up your desk or your life. Instead, it is intended to be a reflection on what is already occurring in each of our lives and a reminder to *flow with* the current, not against it.

Life is not predictable—in fact, the only predictable aspect of life is its sheer unpredictability. Life is not a machine in which every part needs to be well oiled in order to function. Such an "old world" view no longer serves a quantum interpretation of a world in which everything is constantly changing, fiercely connected, and infinitely more interesting than we ever imagined. *In a universe where interdependence is the essence of all life, the relationship between our selves, others and our work is who we are.* Each is connected, affected, influenced, and/or changed by the other. We cannot successfully place aspects of our lives into many bowls, as if our existence were a grand feast. We are instead a cosmic soup, and every aspect of who we are is cooking in one pot.

Once we understand that the "different lives" of self-care, relationships and work are actually only *one* life that we have been given to enjoy, we can begin to see that life as a lovely, intricately woven, and seamless tapestry. Unlike a patchwork quilt, our lives *can* be seamless—flowing *into* and intertwining *with* the many colors, textures, and patterns of one fabric. *Living simultaneously* honors this interconnectedness, and develops fresh ways of integrating the notion that we can live *all aspects* of one life *at the same time.*

As I sit at my computer and write these words, I wonder if this is all actually true, yet the worlds of self-care, personal relationships and work merge with ease without any attempt on my part. Synchronistically, the phone just rang. It is a friend, who has decided to divorce after 13 years of marriage. We talk for 45 minutes, and I listen to her reflect on key personal issues illuminated for me by my own divorce 11 years ago; I know the pain she is feeling because I have experienced it. Instead of this phone call being an interruption to the deadline for a magazine article (only hours away), it becomes a part of what I am suggesting within this book.

Work and relationship flow together; one does not exist without the other. As I complete this sentence, my golden retriever comes to my side for a scratch, just to let me know that he is available if I want to spend more time with him. I feel full of energy on this beautiful weekend morning because of the time I spent earlier reading, then exercising at the health club. Lunch, a nap and garden work are next. My Saturday time-alone only makes the thought of tomorrow afternoon's reunion with friends and work associates even more wonderful. The fabric of self-care, work, and relationships is seamless and simultaneous.

This book is designed with the concept of *flow* in mind, proceeding continuously and smoothly throughout the life-experience—creating, dying, and recreating as a natural process. With this in mind, even the management of time becomes simpler, for when we are in the *flow* of time, present time seems to slow down while time past and time future fade in importance. If we are to bloom into the fullness of our potential over time, using the natural flow of the universe within our individual lives keeps us aligned with creation rather than at odds with it.

You can enter this book wherever you want, whenever you want. If your work is in question, start there. If you are struggling with personal relationships, that may be your beginning point. Or if you have forgotten to include the all-important self in the equation of life-balance, then perhaps self-care is your starting point. Wherever you enter this life-stream, flow with the current and be open to the possibility that "where we are is where we are supposed to be."

Code of the Soul

Perhaps the reason we are interested in this subject of life-balance is that it is the code of our soul to play, laugh, create, and live a fully expressed life. It is the way of the universe to be open, flowing, creative, and expressive, and we are a product of that same code.

As a trainer and workshop leader in both the public and private sector, I see a yearning for much more than business skills in the eyes of thousands of people each year. Souls are malnourished and people are hungry. Although it is sometimes difficult for them to articulate what they are missing, they know it has something to do with wanting a life in balance, having more time and making a difference with their lives. I remind them that we are all on a journey, and there are four particular tools required for the pathway ahead.

Courage 🕱 It takes courage to uncover the code of our individual soul. It requires taking the time to sit in silence and solitude, to reflect upon what barriers stand in the way of simultaneous living, and what we must change, in order to glide rather than shuffle or side-step through life. It might mean stepping outside the comfortable envelope of a lifestyle that contributes to the soul's malnourishment. Living simultaneously is neither for the weak-hearted nor the half-hearted—it is for the full-hearted.

Patience and Persistence 🕱 Patience and persistence are required for this work because this journey is not completed overnight; it is life-long. Being patient with ourselves and others as we stretch and struggle into the fullness of life, while at the same time growing older, is a characteristic of the kind of life that I would like to live. Persistence is necessary if we are committed to *flow* when the journey gets too rough or unpleasant.

Humor 🕱 Along this path (onto which we are all invited), we will hear the stories of others who have learned the art of simultaneous living. We will discover that humor is a necessary antidote to the hard work of listening to the soul and acting upon the wisdom learned. Without laughter, life becomes solemn. While life is serious business, it does not have to be somber business. When we have lost our sense of humor, we have lost touch with the Divine. One good belly laugh can bring a touch of the holy to what otherwise can be difficult and challenging.

Imagination 🕱 *Living simultaneously* also invites imagination. As a wall plaque in my office says, "*Imagination is evidence of the Divine.*" With imagination, we find fresh images and metaphors that help define our experience. With imagination, we cultivate attitudes and visions of how life can be, as well as celebrate life as it is. With imagination, we take a step closer to the source of all creativity—the Divine within each of us.

The Triquetra

This sacred work requires a sacred symbol to inspire us along our journey. The Triquetra is an ancient symbol for the interconnectedness of all life. This ancient Greek symbol first appeared on the coins of Aspendus in Pamphilia. Its three-legged movement, known as "swift feet," throughout antiquity represented the rising of the sun, the phases of the moon and the mystery of the Trinity—all symbols of the renewal of life. The sacred Triquetra is composed of three circles intertwined in such a way as to overlap, while creating a center point. It moves upward while simultaneously flowing downward, outward yet inward.

Interconnectedness is life's creative way; inseparability and union remind us of our relationship to the whole. Thus, the Triquetra is a symbol for the mind's eye, for expressing the sacred foundation of all things created. *Living simultaneously* means flowing with all things . . . upward, downward, inward, and outward. And although we have the multiple components of our busy lives, they are ultimately all one life.

Three Life Circles

The Triad, or force of three, governs the nature of all human experience. Like a three-legged stool, stability requires the magic of three. All events have a positive component, a negative component, and a neutral component that represents a resolution to the conflict. Each component encourages the other to change and thus creates the play of life-experience.

In the formation of the universe, several dynamics were at play. **Matter,** atoms containing protons (positive) and electrons (negative) and **antimatter,** the opposite—protons (negative) and electrons (positive) became a reality less than one-trillionth of a second after the universal "Big Bang" occurred. Because matter and antimatter have equal and opposite characteristics, the universe should have cancelled itself out within the first second after its birth. Obviously it did not, and you and I are proof that for some still-unknown reason, the positive protons in the atomic nucleus triumphed over their negative twin, and created what we refer to as life. In terms of modern physics, life is in violation of the law of symmetry and *if* perfect order had its way, we should not be here. I thank the Divine Creator for the third position.

The number three in mathematics is the approximation of *pi*, the area of a circle—the ratio of the perimeter to its diameter. The circle is as close to perfection as we have found, and therefore has become known as the symbol of wholeness. All other symbols and geometries reflect various aspects of the profound and consummate perfection of the circle. Being a two-dimensional shadow of the sphere, the circle represents all atoms, cells, seeds, planets, star systems, and echoes the total inclusiveness of the Universe. The circle reminds us of the hologram of which we are an integral part. It symbolizes the underlying principle of quantum physics, the inseparable relationship of the part to the whole. This principle of oneness underlies the geometry that is intrinsic in all forms. We are a part of all things and all things are a part of us.

You will find this work composed of circles—*three circles,* each with three circles within those three circles. *Living simultaneously* is about flowing with and through our life-circles as the sacred geometry of our lives. The circles embrace the "perfect three" of flowing from creation to conflict to fulfillment, from expression to regression to re-creation. They represent the process of life and show each of us how we can embrace the simultaneous living that is already within us.

Perhaps now is the time to follow our deep yearning—the yearning to play, to laugh, to create a new picture of how we want to spend the rest of our lives. With good choices and a willingness to flow with the circles of our lives, we may, in fact, leave the legacy of having lived simultaneously.

Welcome to the journey that is already in progress . . .

CIRCLE ONE

Self-Care

Weaving the Seamless Fabric of Awakened Body,
Mystical Mind, and Sacred Spirit

There is a dream dreaming us.

"There is a dream dreaming us," an Australian Bushman once told anthropologist Lauren Van der Post. We *are* a dream, and the dream that dreams us envisions us as our perfect and most complete, wonderful selves. The dream has no limitations, no liabilities. We are wholly known, wholly loved, and completely accepted and understood. As in any dream, we can move with ease and at will, experience a full range of emotions and achieve almost unimaginable goals. When, in our conscious state, we become aware of this dream, we can become a part of the vision and a part of the *One* who dreams us. We become co-creators, evoking the potential of a most perfect and complete life.

One of the most common misnomers of today's "new thinking" is that we *create* our reality. Almost every self-help book includes the challenge to create a desired reality through visualization: *if you can see it, you will become it*. According to quantum theorists, this is not correct. We do *not* create reality; instead we invoke the potential for a reality that is already present. That potential lives within the dream that is dreaming us.

I have been blessed to be the father of two daughters. A large part of my parenting has involved an ongoing vision of wonderful, full lives for my girls. Anyone who is also a parent understands this concept of dreaming

I

the best for those we have co-created. We have a picture of wholeness and health for our children that borders on perfection, with the dream that their lives will be rich and blessed. Thus, the idea that there exists a similar love that dreams the best for us ought not to be foreign, and when we acknowledge that dream, we enter into the sacred realm of co-creating the ultimate reality, by releasing the potential that awaits liberation.

This section is about stepping into the dream already "in process." It is a dream about the potential of who we are to become. Creation has had us in mind and heart since the beginning of time, and we live the potential of this dream each moment. Whether or not we are ever to realize this potential is not only a matter of circumstance, it is a matter of choice.

The White Rhinoceros—My Dream

A year ago I dreamt that I walked alone along a secluded country road and was approached from behind by a maroon Cadillac driven by a woman friend who was 15 years deceased. She invited me into her home and showed me a radar screen that indicated "it" was coming. Even though a long distance away, she said that "the White Rhinoceros" was in the area. Feeling that I needed to reach the nearby village for safety, I left her home and began to run along the country road, certain that the Rhino was still some distance away. However, a few hundred yards along the path, I glanced toward a thicket of trees beside me, and there stood this huge, motionless Rhino, staring at me. I felt panic at its imposing presence, knowing I could not escape. Instead of attempting to flee, I stood and watched while it observed me. Nearby, a Clydesdale horse was tethered to a stake, frantically trying to free itself and escape, while in the distance, a large crowd of people at a soccer game cheered wildly. Unlike the horse or myself, they were completely unaware of the White Rhinoceros' presence, and continued their activity.

It was then that I awoke.

The Interpretation

I sought assistance from a dream therapist to interpret the dream's message. Walking the country road alone is walking one's personal life-path. The entrance of a car from behind—a powerful vehicle of regal color and driven by a gentle messenger—was a message rising up from my subconscious. Alice, the driver of the car, had been a wonderful, elderly friend with whom I had spent many hours in conversation in years past. If anyone were to deliver a message of importance, she would be one to whom I would listen. And just as the messenger was from another dimension, the radar suggested that the message itself was also from above and beyond.

The white rhinoceros is a rare and unusual beast that resides in another part of the world, yet was coming to me. In mythology, the white rhino is known for its magical powers, the color white symbolizing Spirit, and its horn is said to be able to neutralize deadly poison. I was not to stay within the home of the messenger but was instead to seek the protection of a community in the village nearby. I began again to travel the road alone, risking the rhino finding me. The tethered horse represents the emotions, and the sports crowd represents my past practice of being unaware of the presence of the message. Although I felt some panic, I remained calm as I watched the white rhinoceros watch me, because I knew that I could not escape its watchful gaze. I had encountered my most authentic self. I was engaged in soul work and it was my soul that was calling me to change some parts of my life and live out my full potential. Three "learnings" required my attention:

- ⊠ Wake up my sleeping self;
- ⊠ ponder the meaning of the dream; and
- ⊠ effect change.

The Application

If I were to embrace the gift of life-balance, I could not tether my emotional self, nor could I hang out in the crowd of the unconscious. I could not remain within the safe confines of the messenger's home or surround myself with the protection of a village. To encounter my soul, I had to continue my journey in the woods *alone*, unprotected and vulnerable. The white rhino did not come to destroy me but rather to remind me that balance is a rare, yet universal principle that must be the practice of every day. It is not another goal to achieve; it is a state of being, a way of life, a learning how to flow. It is a potential that already resides within our souls, and its release is the way to the path of a life expressed fully and simultaneously.

3

The Quantum Self

If we seek to understand our lives as straight lines or in "five-year plans," the Universe will not cooperate. As Carl Sagan said, "The universe is not required to be in perfect harmony with human ambition." While the human being plans, organizes, and compartmentalizes, attempting some semblance of order and control, the Universe casually continues *its* ongoing dance between chaos and stability, flowing from one to the next and then back again. If we build ways to resist change and to hold on to what is past, our effort is in vain, since life changes with the inward and outward flow of each breath. Therefore, if we really want to understand our lives, we must look for nonlinear patterns that flow through the three circles of our lives (Self-Care, Personal Relationships and Work) and flow with them. Despite what feels like disorder, there *is* some orderly pattern. If you feel as if you have only order and control in your very regularized life, you probably will not be reading this book, AND you can be assured that there is disorder only a breath away.

The quantum theorist Edward Lorenz determined that the path of a particle is in a constant state of motion, yet stays within a bounded, chaotically defined region. Lorenz determined that although the particle appears to move at random, it also obeys a deeper order, thus supporting the idea that order exists within disorder and disorder within order. Could that *deeper order* be *the dream dreaming us,* which allows for the constant motion of flow within the chaotically defined region we call life?

Mechanistic theory, with its deep and pervasive roots, balks at such a suggestion. Appearing as early as the year 5 BC, in the ideas of Greek atomists Semocritus and Leucippus, the concept of a divided universe became the norm for all civilizations that followed. Although they were super-conscious of the varying aspects of body, mind and spirit, the ancient Greeks compartmentalized their functions. They attributed thinking to the brain, emotions to the heart, and wisdom to the soul, and often portrayed these functions as being at war with one another in an attempt to obtain control of the human psyche. Emotions were considered a negative force, and Plato even referred to them as "wild horses" that could lead us astray. Similarly, religious traditions saw the emotions and the mind as paths to temptation and sin. A similar understanding prevails even today.

This *vision of division* influenced scientific thought and may have found its fullest expression in the ideology of Sir Isaac Newton. Newton conceptualized the universe as a celestial machine in which human beings were only one cog in the grander wheel. Philosopher René Descartes was successful in separating the worlds of science and theology into two distinct and unrelated realms. And so the story developed. We began to understand political systems mechanistically, and the divisional system found its way into every form of organization. Corporations, religious, or social systems were not immune to this imposing force. Even as conventional wisdom suggests that *a house divided will soon fall,* we have successfully perpetuated this vision of separation.

Conversely, to be successful in sports, players must learn the power of unity. Families, neighborhoods, and organizations that function as a whole, instead of as "rugged individuals," know the power of "being one." Although separateness is a necessary step in individuation and toward becoming self-aware, it is a stage of childhood and adolescence. In maturity, the Quantum Self departs from this thinking and focuses on the whole, not the parts.

In the following sections, the unbalanced self follows a three-part process toward the ultimate in Self-Care, becoming a Quantum person. Part one is to first awaken from the sleep-state through the heightened sensitivity of the body's Erotic Intelligence. Once awake, the power of the Mystical Mind unifies the realms of thinking and feeling into a coherent process for the purpose of listening, pondering and learning from the meaning of life metaphors and stories. From the wisdom discerned, the energy of Sacred Spirit moves the changing self toward the gift of freedom that results from a life in fullness and personal balance.

☒ AWAKENED BODY — EROTIC INTELLIGENCE

The world only makes sense when the senses make love. —SAM KEEN

The body is a mini-universe—a perfect example of a whole being composed of the sum of its parts, and an organism that flows beautifully. We entertain as much space between atomic particles within us as the Universe's space between galaxies. Made up of the same galactic material as the stars, we also flow, change, expand, create, and die; we are a tiny, yet integral part of a much grander picture. On a physical level, the body works continuously toward balance—balancing chemistry, temperature, pressure, ingestion, digestion, et cetera. The moment imbalance appears, alarms go off and multiple armies rush to the scene to begin repair.

Our quality of life is directly related to our level of consciousness. As suggested by the Delphic Oracle, "Know Thyself" is an essential process, for a lack of inner knowing often creates a sense of dread and a fear of being. As the end of the millennium approached, how many delighted in the drama of imagining the end of life and expecting the worst—all because we have merely orbited the sun one more time? Most likely such thinkers have lived their lives much the same way.

We live in a world that changes so quickly it is imperative to learn how to reformulate consciousness. Consciousness cannot be institutionalized or routinized. Like the wind, consciousness must be "in process," for without movement, it becomes stagnant air. Sigmund Freud sought to liberate the ego from stale ideology just as Karl Marx attempted to free consciousness from what he perceived as a repressive economic system. If Jesus Christ had lived in the Dark Ages, his attempt to free the restrictive consciousness of the Catholic Church might well have brought him to the cross numerous times.

How do we awaken ourselves from our slumber when it is so tempting to "nap" through half of life? Our marvelous five senses provide such a capability through what I refer to as *Erotic Intelligence*. If we were to slumber through the beginning of a fire, we would eventually be alerted by the pungent *smell* of smoke, *hear* the crackling of flame, *feel* the heat of the fire, *taste* the smudge of ash lingering in the thick air, and eventually *see* the consuming force. We can all benefit from a periodic internal fire to awaken our souls to the richer potential that is within us.

An Example

Twice within the past month I have had an accident on my bicycle. I just took up this sport within the last year, after ruining my knees with too many years of running, so I must claim some innocence due to lack of experience. These are not the kinds of accidents that one would normally talk about—not like cocktail chatter about "near death" experiences. In fact, these accidents were so embarrassing that most people would be smart

6

enough to remain silent about them. However, being an extrovert, I am compelled to share my mishaps. In my opinion, whoever invented toe clips for bicycle pedals should be subjected to intense interrogation as to why. As for anyone who purchases them and has them installed on his or her bicycle, I have three words of advice: *seek professional help!* Here is what happened.

While descending a large hill, an inevitable equal-and-opposite reaction lay ahead—an *ascending* hill. Between these two opposing forces was (to my mind) a misplaced stoplight, where nine cars foolishly sat wasting fuel. My inclination was not to join this inert group of vehicles, but instead to coast carefully through the intersection and use my newly acquired speed to attack the upcoming hill. However, wisdom (and traffic laws) prevailed.

Slowly coming to a near stop, I thought I might be able to balance just long enough for the light to change, but it didn't. Forced to come to a complete stop, my brain communicated to my body to get off the bike, and *quickly.* Every part got the message except my feet, which were still locked in position in the toe clips, apparently either unable or unwilling to release themselves. Sudden horror flooded my consciousness, then reality hit me: I was going down—in full view of nine cars filled with passengers.

At lightning speed, all my Erotic Intelligence awakened, and at the same time—almost as if in slow motion—I could somehow *see* the amused gaze in the eyes of those viewing from the waiting cars, while I also watched the ground rise toward me at what seemed to be supersonic speed; I *smelled* the scent of California anise, an aromatic weed growing wild at roadside, even as I smelled my own pungent, fear-driven sweat. I could easily *hear* the sound of irreverent language coming from my mouth as it offered an apt description of my bike, my toes, and my stupidity. I could almost *taste* the embarrassment of all this, and it was then that I was *touched* by the experience as all my 200 pounds landed on one elbow. Then it was over. There I was, in full view of nearly 15 amused onlookers—equipment scattered all over the road, but with my feet still proudly clipped in place. Another biker who managed to execute the light change perfectly, glided by and expressed his kind sympathy with one word: "Bummer."

Now what did I learn from such an experience? Nothing. Two weeks later, it happened again, but that time, at least I fell on my *other* elbow. Then I got it. *"As you slow down, disengage your feet from the toe clips prior to stopping."* If only the *rest* of life's lessons could be learned so easily. Erotic Intelligence serves to guide us in this pursuit, and becomes the superhighway to our conscious self. While our senses drink in information, collect data in an attempt to awaken us from our perpetual tendency to "sleep" and thereby miss the parade, Erotic Intelligence helps us begin the process of awakening from the dream.

STORIES OF EROTIC INTELLIGENCE

Aunt Nellie

My grandmother had one sister who lived with her when I was a child. We called her "Aunt Nellie," probably because that was her name—but more than that, she really *was* an Aunt Nellie. To begin with, she *looked* the part. There was one chair in the middle of the living room where she always sat, and I mean *always*. I can never recall a time when I visited my grandmother that Nellie was not plopped in "her" chair, the image of which created a rather frightening sight for a young boy. With her large body wedged into her "throne," she would somehow chew on the side of her tongue and smoke cigarettes at the same time. My dear, but rather proper grandmother must have just abhorred this presence, but "family was family"—at least back then.

I do not remember Aunt Nellie ever saying anything; she just grunted and made animal-type sounds. These sounds seemed to emerge deep from the bowels of her massive frame, and always scared me to death. If I had to use the bathroom—and this would be only when I was desperate—I had to make my way past "the chair" and risk being grabbed or eaten by this frightening character. As a consequence, I developed strong bladder skills in those early years.

The most memorable of all Aunt Nellie's attributes was the smell associated with her. Never could the term "pure-fume" be associated with this lady of leisure: she reeked of a fragrance that was a combination of stale cigarettes and the scent of a body that seldom moved. And, not surprisingly, so reeked "the chair." When the inevitable occurred and Nellie was called to a "higher" chair, the "lower chair" still remained in my grandmother's living room. Perhaps it was sentiment. Perhaps my grandmother actually missed her sister, my rather beastly aunt. Whatever it was, "the chair" remained, almost as if an altar for what *not* to become. In spite of her physical absence, Nellie's aroma lingered. Even though I began to enjoy the luxury of using my grandmother's bathroom without fear, the fragrance still emanated so strongly from "the chair" that it made me look twice to see if she really *was* gone.

Interestingly enough, even as I write these words, I catch a whiff of Aunt Nellie. The memory of her is everlasting, but always startling when it resurfaces. Perhaps she is visiting from the other realm just to protest this public revelation. Or maybe I have been sitting in front of this computer for too long in *this* "chair." Maybe my dog Bear needs a bath or my sweat clothes—which are donned in the dark early morning hours for writing—need to be tossed into the washing machine. Whatever just occurred, my Erotic Intelligence has reminded me of the wondrous ability of our senses to bring us back, to lead us forward, and to awaken us to the "pure-fumes" of every day.

Learning how to incorporate scent into our daily lives is an important step in our awakening. We learn which scent relaxes us, which gives us balance, which gives us energy. Ritualistically, every Saturday morning I go to a Farmer's Market to purchase a week's worth of fresh-cut flowers. My kitchen becomes a flower shop as I create five different arrangements that will grace my home throughout the week; star lilies and tuber rose are favorites, since they easily fill the house with their sweet fragrance.

Taking the time to *smell* the spray starch, however is just as important as smelling the roses. I associate spray starch with being loved, just as the smell of coconut oil reminds me of time spent relaxing on a beach. When we use our ability to smell as a way of awakening, there is no end to what our Erotic Intelligence can provide. *Noticing* my neighbor's new haircut or the ever-increasing quince on a roadside tree is equal to paying attention to the necessary details of every day. *Hearing* the sounds of silence in between the notes of a sonata is as thrilling as the sound of my children's voices when they call me collect. *Tasting* the sweetness of a great Cabernet wine is like a delicious kiss, and *feeling* the warmth of a lingering hug is equal to a roaring fire on a rainy night. Thank you, Aunt Nellie—for without you, the intelligence of my senses would not be quite the same.

Georgia

Georgia became pregnant at the age of 14. Since many in our society deemed this morally unacceptable, she was isolated by her predicament. She sought the assistance of an adoption agency to make plans for the child's delivery, as well as help in finding a home for her baby. Unable to depend upon her mother—who not only worked three jobs but was also completely unaware of this well-kept secret—Georgia traveled this path alone and afraid. When the time came for her to give birth, she took a bus to the center where she was to deliver her child—a child who would soon after bless the lives of a young couple unable to conceive a child of their own.

The delivery was difficult, during which Georgia screamed away some of her guilt and shame that were far more painful for her than the actual act of giving birth. With the child's birth, she had hoped she could "get on" with her life and return to being a regular, yet much wiser 14-year-old. But then it happened: she *saw* him; she *heard* his cry; she *smelled* her own blood that covered him. As she reached out for him, the midwife placed the squealing infant into her arms, and at that moment, everything changed. This was *her* child, *her* baby—a creation made out of *her* very cells . . . *her* blood . . . *her* being. She was a mother, and he was her baby. As she *held* the child close to her breast, *tasting* the sweetness of the moment, he quieted and fell asleep.

Georgia's mind began to race as she thought, how could she keep this child? How could she tell her still-unaware mother? What would she do to support him? Knowing that these thoughts were not rational, she was overwhelmed with despair. She had made a promise, she had even signed an agreement to relinquish the child after birth. She had given up the right to be her child's mother—to watch him grow and to nourish him with her love. She then began to sob so hard that she awakened her son, who joined in the symphony of sorrow.

The exchange was rather simple from an outsider's viewpoint. Georgia gave her child to an attendant, then she took a shower, was checked out by a physician and given money for a cab ride home. It was over. She had put a troubling life-chapter behind her and in so doing, had given an incredible gift to a young couple. She wondered, would they love him as she would have? She would never know, but she had to assure herself that they would.

As she walked toward the waiting taxi, she experienced a feeling of great insignificance. She had merely been a vehicle for someone else's joy. Like a garbage can that held the remains of a once-great dinner party, Georgia felt spent, unappreciated, and demoralized by her "gift-giving." She went home and crawled under the covers, where she cried many more tears.

The story does not end here, because Georgia was *not* your average 14-year-old. Pondering the pain and demoralization she felt, she knew how others must have felt as well, when enduring the insensitivity of such a sterile process. So she set out to devise a way of changing the process. Today, that childbirth center has a very different ritual for completing the birth and subsequent adoption process.

The biological mother becomes the center of a circle where everyone participates. The circle includes the mother and her child, the family of the mother, the adopting family, the medical staff, and agency personnel. With the mother and child in the circle's center, every other member of the circle has the opportunity to express appreciation to the mother for the gift that she has created. The mother has the same opportunity to share with others what this process has meant to her and what her wishes are for her child. The child is eventually and ceremoniously handed from the arms of the biological mother into the waiting arms of the adoptive family. Applause and signs of appreciation follow, and the adoptive family is blessed for the challenges of parenting that lie ahead. A brief reception follows, then people depart, everyone's life goes on.

Where would that center be today without the Erotic Intelligence of that young mother? Her senses awakened her to a fire within that would not be quenched by the typically sterile routine. She wanted more, and so she created it.

Alice

The William Butler Yeats poem that follows concerns a time when, in the unlikeliest of places and at a most unpredictable time, he encountered the holiest of holies:

> *My fiftieth year had come and gone*
> *I sat a solitary man in a crowded London shop,*
> *An open book and empty cup on the marble table top.*
> *While on the shop and street I gazed*
> *My body, of a sudden, blazed*
> *And twenty minutes, more or less*
> *It seemed so great my happiness,*
> *That I was blessed and could bless.*

And so it was with Alice.

One of the most powerful awakenings of my life occurred at a hospital bedside in the small village of Bethany, several miles outside Jerusalem, Israel. In 1982, I was on a personal quest to experience God in a land considered "holy" by three world religions. Like any tourist, I visited all the "must-see" spots, looking for whatever it was that I was seeking. Unfortunately, what I first discovered was the visual clutter of memorabilia salespeople hawking "Empty Tomb T-Shirts" or "Wailing Wall Watches." These "lasting reminders" of The Holy Land were a true testimony to the acrimonious power of capitalism and its ability to infiltrate every nook and cranny of a potential market. Although the ancient city of Jerusalem was most stimulating—with open markets and thousands of intriguing people milling through narrow, hallowed streets—I could not feel what it was that I sought to experience. My personal faith wanted renewal and my spirit needed a jolt, yet such an encounter with the Almighty was escaping my sensual grasp. At least until Bethany.

Walking the two-mile road to this ancient town, I recalled that Bethany had been the home to the Biblical Lazarus—another human being who required an awakening from a permanent grip of unconsciousness. Arriving at the outskirts of town, I eventually found my way to the intended object of my visit, a hospital where a woman named Alice had been a patient for 18 years. Because I had donated money to the all-encompassing work of this hospital (that also served as an orphanage and home for unwed mothers), the hospital's director wanted to thank me personally, and entertain me for lunch. However, first she asked that I visit Alice, one of the hospital's longest-term patients who had indicated that she wanted to meet me.

Making my way down a long, dark hallway toward Alice's room, I was moved by the sight of many children—all of them sitting on the floor and leaning against the wall while eating a most unsavory-looking gruel for their midday meal. My Erotic Intelligence was on full alert since I did not care for either the smell or the sight of this house of refuge on just an average day.

As I was led into a small room at the end of the hallway, my first impression was that of a single, bare light-bulb, hanging from the ceiling on an exposed wire. While certainly a dramatic departure from the quality of health care we in the Western world have come to expect, this dark and dank room also had a small window that invited in some natural light. Under that window, in the bed where she had been for 18 years, lay Alice.

My first reaction was one of shock at the sight of Alice, who had only half a body—both of her legs had been severed in an accident many years earlier. Instinctively, I made my way toward her, even as every fiber of my being wanted to bolt. As I approached her bed, she extended her hand in greeting and said, "Oh Jeff, it is so good to meet you." Taking her thin-yet-strong hand, I began to formulate a cordial response, but before I could return the greeting she asked, "May I sing for you?" Once again startled, and confused by such a confrontation, I managed to utter some nearly unintelligible response that must have sounded like "yes."

With the go-ahead, Alice began to sing. Contrary to what I expected, one of the purest sounds I have ever heard began to emerge from her half-body. She brought into this darkened room a quality of music that seemed to come from another realm. The words were simple, yet they still remain in my mind to this day. They were a prayer of thanksgiving for how blessed her life had been and an expression of the gratitude she felt for her hospital home and her family of patients residing there. Although my natural inclination was to thank her for her song and ignore what seemed to be the ludicrous nature of this event, I instead began to weep. Unable to control the well of emotion that began to fill me, my weeping reached a level so deep that it felt as if it were an outpouring of every ounce of judgment and cynicism I had ever entertained. I began to feel as pure as the songbird who had rejoiced, who now offered no response to my weeping except a loving gaze.

Why had this occurred? What was the reason for this uncharacteristic emotional display from me, in front of two people whom I had met only minutes earlier? The reality that suddenly came crashing into my awareness—like a 747 landing on my roof top—was that I was standing in the presence of God. Residing within this frail being, who exhibited more patience and joy than anyone I had ever encountered, was the very spirit that I sought. The paradox itself became humorous. Despite all my efforts to find the Divine in the Holy Land through weeks of investigating holy ground, I became keenly aware that the Divine was neither confined in expectation nor corralled in monuments of the past, but was more often discovered in the most unlikely places, at the most unlikely times, and in the most unusual of characters.

Awakened Body: Making Love, Making Sense

The notion that *the world only makes sense when the senses make love* suggests an inter-relatedness of all functions—the communication between mind, body and spirit and what happens when they flow together as one. Imagine hearing the beauty of a flaming sunset, tasting the warmth of a long hug, seeing the deliciousness of roasted garlic, smelling a Mozart concerto, or feeling the bouquet of an aging Cabernet wine. When we awaken to these possibilities, life becomes even more full.

Making love with intimacy is one of the deepest expressions of self-care, that climaxes with the experience of a holy encounter. A healing act, a form of art, a way to play and a way to deepen the spirit within—all of our senses work simultaneously to bring us to the door of the Divine as we shout, "Oh God," as our way of saying thank you. In climax, we taste the sweetness of fulfillment, hear the sounds of merging hearts, feel the beauty of acceptance, and we see what life in fullness can be like as we touch the hand of Divine expression. Making love allows us to make sense of the world in a new way.

If we were to live our lives in the same way that our bodies function naturally, we would more often awaken to the possibility of each moment and make love with life itself. Erotic Intelligence sends the signal that our lover is on the doorstep of each opportunity as we open our arms and await a full embrace.

⊠ MYSTICAL MIND — COHERENCE

Awe is the beginning of wisdom. —ABRAHAM HESCHEL

If awe is the beginning of wisdom, as Rabbi Heschel suggests, then wisdom must be the culmination of awe. Just as awakening from the dream is the beginning of life-changing action, then action itself must be the culmination of the awakening. One without the other resembles a dangling participle—an incomplete thought form; the components work and "stick" together like a peanut-butter-and-jelly sandwich. The state of "sticking together" is coherence—a natural or logical connection that is both consistent and congruent.

The latest research in neuroscience confirms that emotion and cognition are interacting, coherent functions, each with its own unique type of intelligence. When these functions are out-of-phase, overall awareness is reduced and conversely, when they are in sync, awareness is expanded. Our mental clarity, reaction time, vision, listening abilities, feelings, and sensitivities are all affected by the degree of mental and emotional coherence we experience. What results from coherence are a *Feeling Mind* and a *Thinking Heart*. Each is connected to the other, and each influences the other's actions. For example, research has proven the critical importance of emotions in the decision-making process. People who have experienced brain damage in the area of the brain that integrates the emotional and cognitive systems can no longer function effectively day-to-day, even though their mental abilities are normal. In the physiologically healthy and awakened self, *Thinking Heart* and *Feeling Mind* unite together to make wise choices and good decisions.

But what is the process occurring *between* these two functions that determines the best outcome? As with any beginning and ending, there must be a middle space between two ends. With the coherence of emotion and cognition, something must happen in the middle to produce wisdom. I suggest that this space (or process) is a factor rare to many, yet essential for living simultaneously—*silence*. It is silence that provides space for our intellect and our hearts to become one, for producing the ultimate outcome—wisdom.

In the cycle of human growth, we do not consider our lives as a beginning and an end. Instead we categorize ourselves into at least, three phases: child, adult, and elder—the beginning, the middle, and the end. I find it even more interesting to assign three archetypal characters to these three phases: the Mystic, the Master, and the Mentor—and then blend them into one creation, Mystical Mind.

We begin the cycle with the beauty of the Mystical Child whose heart has the capacity for awe; every object or event becomes a possibility for inquiry and/or wonder. The cycle is completed in the Elder/Mentor whose voice speaks with the wisdom of words and the patience of his or her soul. The wisdom of the Elder/Mentor fully completes the circle that began with the awe of the Mystical Child, but not without the action of the Master in the middle. The mastery of the young adult contributes to the mind's creativity, flowing with purpose and fueling a life without reservation; every obstacle becomes an opportunity for growth, achievement, and fulfilling life-purpose. However, it is only while practicing silence that the

Master can ponder the meaning of these lessons learned from awe. It is also through this practice that the three characters can unite, to become the one Mystical Mind.

I practice a particular method for unifying the three aspects of life-stages. I imagine my childhood heart exploring the woods behind my family's former home and ponder—in silence—about the hills and trees and tiny streams. It was with awe that I used to observe the beauty of the evening stars that seemed to shine more clearly over the small Upstate New York town where I lived. Then I picture Jeff—the adult—as one who believes that everything is possible and lives by the motto, "Let's do it." But this picture also includes a man of silent spaces, who sometimes spends hours in solitude, while pondering the meaning of metaphors, or listening to the power of another's story and noting the lessons learned through the process. And Jeffrey "the Elder" is a man of gentle strength whose smile is deeply etched into his eyes, suggesting a mood of joy and peace. These three figures then merge into one—one-in-three and three-in-one: a re-creation of our own holy trinity—coherence; sticking together; unity—the Mystical Mind.

Silence

> *The endless cycle of ideas and action,*
> *Endless invention, endless experiment,*
> *Brings knowledge of motion but not of stillness;*
> *Knowledge of speech, but not of silence;*
> *Knowledge of words, and ignorance of the Word.*
> *All of our knowledge brings us nearer to death,*
> *But nearness to death no nearer to God.*
> *Where is the Life we have lost in living?*
> *Where is the wisdom we have lost in knowledge?*
> *Where is the knowledge we have lost in information?*
>
> (T.S. ELLIOT, "Choruses from The Rock")

Silence is an essential practice for living simultaneously. We can fully enjoy the wonders of the Mystical Mind only when we make the time to meld the facilities of emotion and cognition for the nurturing of wisdom. Without silence, "wisdom is lost in knowledge, knowledge is lost in information."

I have always struggled with silence. I am an extrovert and, like all extroverts, I need to talk in order to process what I am thinking. I was taught some years ago that there really are only three personal practices that are required for a fulfilling life: sit quietly, love your family and do what needs to be done. I have always tried to follow this very practical life guide which is rooted in the challenge of silence.

Due to being "silence-challenged," I have made extra efforts to develop a contemplative practice. Fifteen years ago I started a six-week sabbatical with the intention of beginning with a week—in silence—at a Camaldalese Monastery near Big Sur, California.

Leaving behind all the details of a very busy life, I happily drove southward from my home to begin this journey of silence and reflection with the notion of achieving peace and solitude. Sustained periods of silence were unfamiliar to me, and it would be more than challenging to live among monks for whom silence was a way of life. A quieter life seemed to call me, and I was responding. However, Mother Nature had other plans: one of the worst storms to hit California in over 100 years raged as I traveled south along the beautiful-but-precarious coastal route. Although it started as a very typical winter storm, it soon matured into a torrential rain-and windstorm that pelted the coastline with unimaginable fury. Committed to my goal, however, I continued onward. As I turned one of the myriad sharp corners that encompass that route, a wave suddenly came across the highway that normally only offers a perpetual ocean *view*. As the wave of water washed across the front of my car I thought, "This can't get any worse." It did.

Just then, the hill to my left—once a strong, proud, upright collection of stone and gravel—suddenly became mush, and slid downward. As I looked into my rearview mirror, the roadway where I had been only seconds earlier was now a slush farm. Halfway to my destination, I pressed on—only to encounter three miles later the first of several "ROAD CLOSED" signs, complete with flashing lights. Knowing what I had just left behind me, I was forced to continue forward. Miraculously, I arrived at the Hermitage and Brother Isaiah, the only monk allowed to speak, welcomed me with, "I can't believe you made it!" "Oh, Great," I thought, "a doubting Monk."

Escorted to the "cell" where I would stay, I ate a light dinner and waited for the height of the storm to hit. With 100-m.p.h. winds battering my tiny cabin, it was easy to imagine the plate-glass window that faced the ocean shattering and decapitating me in the middle of the night. Not wanting to lose that member of my collective parts, I did what any courageous person seeking silence would do—I slept in the windowless bathroom. Just as I got comfortable somewhere between the toilet and the sink, a tree decided to visit the "cell" next to mine, making a crashing entrance. This was my first night of peace and relaxation.

The next morning, with Brother Isaiah nowhere to be found, I tried to find out about storm damage from the other monks. They listened intently, bowed politely, and walked by this babbling visitor. Noticing a road-crew at work 1000 feet below this cliffside retreat, I made my way down the tree-strewn roadway. When I reached a crew member standing next to his distinguished Caltrans-orange truck, I asked about the damages. "Pretty bad," he said, "worst I've ever seen." "That was comforting," I thought. Now for the real question: "How long before you think I can drive out of here?" I asked. "Oh, maybe four or five . . . months" he replied, seeming to enjoy the increasing look of fear on my face. "Months?" I replied, loud enough to startle him. "I've got to get out of here by Friday." "Well," he mused, "you *could* walk north about 30 miles." "I could do that," I said, "thirty miles is no big deal." "Of course, you'd have to swim about a mile and a half, where the road dropped into the ocean," he continued, now fully enjoying my increased panic. "What about if I walked south?" I inquired frantically. "Nope, the road is all gone down there."

"There *must* be a way out," I said defiantly. "There is," he said, "if you take that road right over there, up over the mountain and walk to King City. It's pretty clear, except for the one big mud slide." "How big?" I asked. "About 30 feet deep. Course, even if you were lucky enough *not* to disappear into the mud, the wild boars will probably get ya." "Wild boars?" I exclaimed. "Yeah, they travel in packs up there in the mountains, and if they corner ya, they can chew your legs to the bone." That did it. I was finished with this conversation with the Attila-the-Hun of roadwork, who delighted in every second of this roadside torture. Thanking him for his time and sound advice, I headed back up to the retreat center.

Brother Isaiah appeared with a big smile, and asked how I had fared the night. I muttered something resembling civility, and then asked if he knew of a way I could get to Carmel. "Yes," he said. My heart quickened. "Brother Thomas has a dentist appointment in Carmel in August." Since it was then January, the offer was not terribly helpful. Feeling as though I had just signed up for a life sentence, I did what any person trapped in a place committed to silence would do—I made my way to the retreat center's sole public phone.

Why was I having such a difficult time facing the very experience that I thought I was seeking? Had I lived so long in a world of noise that I didn't know how to be silent for a long period without the bliss of interruption? I was troubled by the reality of my stirrings, but I forged on toward freedom.

Twenty phone calls and four days later, I was informed that a helicopter had been enlisted to airlift me out of the center. On Friday morning, as the storm that had started five days earlier finally seemed to be breaking up, I could hear the sound of whirling blades in the distance. As the skies opened up for what seemed like only a few seconds, a helicopter appeared, swooped down into the parking lot, and retrieved me from my respite of peace and solitude. Looking up from the center down below, all the monks waved goodbye and probably broke their silence just long enough to utter, "and good riddance."

How do we practice the lost art of silence in a world that creates so much noise? The task is not easy, but it is essential. Creating silence where noise traditionally lives may mean simply turning off the car radio and basking in the silent space of your mechanical hermitage. It may require finding an empty conference room, closet or bedroom that becomes your own temporary respite and renewal station. It may be that we discover that the background noise of television or radio is not as rewarding a companion as the generous comrade of silence. The call to silence may mean attempting the uncomfortable practice of being alone and forgoing the endless invitations of noise.

Today, I practice silence every day. Such practice has required a change in attitude yet it has become the fuel of my energy and the source of many ideas. It is like a warm bath to an often, tired spirit. This effort is not always easy, yet it is worth every inconvenience, because ultimately, wisdom speaks to the one who remains silent in order to listen.

Listening and Pondering

Assuming that it is possible to be even marginally successful at embracing some semblance of silence in the midst of daily chaos, once achieved, the "container" can be used for listening and pondering—listening to the calling of the Thinking Heart that we often never hear and pondering the messages of the Feeling Mind that we often overlook. Like two lovers whose bodies writhe in a passionate embrace, when listening and pondering are engaged, wisdom is born.

Although we are required to practice listening throughout each day, it does not mean that "practice makes perfect." When we uncover a message buried deep beneath excessive verbiage, it is like discovering a gem hidden deep within the shadow of a cave. It is often hard work, yet it is well worth the effort. We *can* learn to listen to the sounds of life in the same way, for a deeper level of understanding and meaning. Erotic Intelligence indicates that love makes sounds, and distress is audible, as is the blooming of the flower. Pondering is even more foreign to our daily activities, since it requires "considering something deeply and thoroughly, to speculate curiously, to be in awe." Pondering our thoughts and our emotions means that we are so awake that we are able to think, feel, and muse beyond the superficial level most often required of us, thereby entering into the realm of childlike awe. It is from here that we can entertain the future guest, wisdom.

An Example

Aging is a process that we all experience, but some of us do it better than others. Influenced by a deep and dysfunctional mythology about old age in our culture, we seem to do everything to avoid it and little to embrace it. "Flesh-scaping" is an enormous business as we trim, dye, tuck, lift, plug, and scrape away any semblance of age that has taken up residence in our bodies. We are taught that "getting old is bad," and we foolishly believe it. Even though in most cultures the elder is the recipient of the highest esteem and honor, some of the unnecessary stress of our unbalanced lives in Western culture comes from the fear of joining that realm of the esteemed. We can transform such a limiting notion through the art of listening and pondering.

Listening to the wisdom of our bodies is a natural step toward healthful longevity, since this incredible, breathing organism will tell us everything that it needs if we will listen. Just as obvious as hunger and thirst are the needs for touch, release, forgiveness, and gratitude. Our bodies require laughter, dance, song and play almost as much as they need water and nutrients. When our esteem is low, so is our capacity for standing up straight. When we are experiencing completeness, we feel larger than life.

Ability need not be restricted by the accumulation of years, since for some, life begins at 80. The octogenarian who has learned to ponder the meaning of life re-creates his or her body according to the way he or she thinks and feels. I know an 83-year-old rancher who builds stone walls, raises horses, and manages his 100-acre ranch 7 days a week. With a grip that feels as if it could crush my hand, this man knows of no limitation associated with the birth date on his California driver's license.

Constance Nelson was a longtime friend who never stopped learning. At the age of 87, she checked more books out of the library in a month's time than I read in a year. She would entertain me after a weeknight's dinner by playing classical music on the piano. Whenever I had questions ranging from protocol to "how to get wax out of fine linen," Connie was the one to call. She was brilliant, and the only thing to stop her mind from working was the brain tumor that eventually ended her life.

The painter William Lewis started his painting career at the age of 70. Now 83, he paints 12 hours a day, makes his own frames, and enjoys a successful career. As if that weren't enough of an accomplishment, in his "spare time," he wrote *Pictures at an Exhibition*—a wildly humorous and inspirational book about living your dreams no matter what your age. My children's great, great-grandmother, at the age of 102, once said to me, "I just don't know where the day goes. There is just not enough time to get everything done that I want to do." Her varied activities included serving as wise counsel to her many children. At the age of 83, her son Grant met a younger woman of 74 whom he wanted to marry. However, he told his bride-to-be that he couldn't marry her until she met his mother. Some things never change!

When we learn to ponder the meaning of life, aging becomes a beautiful and natural expression of living life fully. The aging process need not surprise us like a thief in the night coming to rob us of our youthfulness; instead, aging is like a rushing stream that becomes a deep and wide river upon which the "great ships" depend.

What other subjects could benefit from our listening and pondering? If we mused over the kind of space we create for relationships, would we help those who know and love us become more autonomous, and more whole, as the result of knowing us? If we listen to and ponder the needs of our often-tired bodies, stressed from the exhausting enterprise of worry, will we give rest and renewal to the form that will carry us well into the next decades? And if we were to discover the coherent voice of wisdom while at work, would our work become our art and would we spend each day contributing to a legacy for positive change?

In the following section, let's ponder three areas that can unveil an uncanny wisdom and a set of learnings for creating the kind of life we all seek: Meaning in Metaphor, Understanding through Story, and Lessons as Guides.

MEANING IN METAPHOR

The universe milks meaning out of metaphor—Holy Cow!
—SAM KEEN

"The metaphor is a device of the poetic imagination—a matter of extraordinary rather than ordinary language. The metaphor is understanding and experiencing one kind of thing in terms of another." (*Metaphors We Live By*—Lakoff and Johnson). *Mystical Mind* is a metaphor. It suggests that the process of decision making involves more than merely depending on limited cognition and emotion, and instead integrates the two centers, creating a new reality of coherence. Through Mystical Mind, we can learn to change what we feel by what we think, and we can learn to change what we think by what we feel. Mystical Mind connects our bodies and brains, our thoughts and our emotions, and creates the possibility of compassion over success, meaning over matter.

Because imagery is such a powerful influence as well as the way in which most of us learn, we are in need of new metaphoric imagery if we are to change the way in which we live. Consider the common metaphor, *Time is Money*: we manage how we *spend* our time, *calculate* what inefficiency *costs* us, determine how we must *budget* our time, what has been *invested* in us, or how we are living on *borrowed* time. It is easy to see how the imagery of this tired metaphor has contributed to the frantic way in which we live our lives. Instead, consider the metaphor, *Time is Precious*: life is a *gift*, our time is *valuable*, minutes are *dear*, our presence is *priceless*, we are *worthy*. With just a bit of adjustment, we can create new meaning.

22

Metaphors of Self

The mind-pictures that we have of ourselves are some of the most powerful pictures for determining how we behave. When we see ourselves as being "out of place," we experience the discomfort of not belonging. When we look at ourselves in the mirror and determine that we are not attractive enough, we experience ourselves in the very same way. Too fat, too thin, too tall, too short—*The Way of Too* again rears its ugly head in the endless list of images for self-criticism.

A vivid experience from my past involved a 17-year-old anorexic girl whom I visited in the hospital. I grew to love this gentle soul whose life was slipping away daily. In spite of intravenous feeding, her body had already "programmed" itself to die, and so she weighed only about 60 pounds. Initially, I did not mention the disease of her mind and body, for that was everyone else's "agenda," and I first wanted to establish a relationship with her soul. We developed a love for each other through our daily conversations. However, feeling great frustration at the eventual loss of this new friend—and for what I thought was an absurd reason—I dared to ask quite vehemently, "Why are you doing this—why are you starving yourself?" She replied quite matter-of-factly, "Because I am too fat."

The power of that negative image drove her behavior and pushed her over the edge of reality, into the abyss of self-delusion. No longer could she distinguish what was real from what was not. She died one month later—paradoxically, when she had no more weight to lose.

One of the most insidious metaphors directing the "program" of too many lives is that of "being small." While training public speakers, we notice that most of them, when called upon to deliver a talk, immediately experience the phenomenon, "Why did I just become so small and how did this room become so large?" In time of fear, we shrink to our smallest self and curl up into a protective position when just the opposite is required.

Five years ago, 12 of us spent a week in Yosemite National Park. On the first night, and seven miles out in the wilderness, a very large and clever bear ripped two of our food packs from a wire hanging 18 feet above the ground. Wisdom determined that a guard should maintain a watch on the boulder directly below the hanging food, so that he or she could frighten the bear away if it should return. The chances of the bear not returning were infinitesimal, while the chances of my being chosen as the first guard were high. Both occurred. As I sat upon that boulder in 28-degree temperature, I could smell the putrid scent of this still-hungry creature as well as hear a deep growling noise. My flashlight, for some reason, chose not to work and I was not a happy camper. Unable to see anything in the pitch-black of the night, I sat frozen in place, realizing that the only thing standing between an 800-pound bear and ten more hanging food sacks was me. Then it happened—the bear disappeared. For some reason, the putrid stench and huffing-and-puffing were gone. Feeling quite proud of my ability to "scare off" this creature, I sat, now quite content to await the arrival of the next guard. After five minutes more on my post, and with everything silent, for some unknown reason, I was inclined to turn and look *behind* me. There it was. The bear had quietly left the front position and gone around the hill to approach the food source from the rear.

Not quite sure *which* was the food source, I did what any courageous camper would do—I panicked. Just as I was having "my problem," the bear decided to raise itself up on its hind legs. As if that were not intimidating enough, this creature now appeared to be at least 12 feet tall. So there we were: little me and the big bear, each interested in the same thing—food. Then it happened. From some extreme corner of the universe (probably from a galaxy far, far away) came some source of power or foolishness that commanded me to do what we had been taught to do in just such circumstances. *Make yourself as big as possible and run toward the bear, yelling.* With every fiber of my being wanting to do just the opposite (except for the yelling part) I instead listened to this "cosmic command" and charged forward. To my great surprise, the bear, fully intimidated by my now-commanding and threatening presence, dropped down on all fours and ran off. "Well, he wasn't so tough," I thought. Swaggering back toward my post and feeling extremely powerful and rugged, I felt nauseated to the extent of almost vomiting. That is a night I will always remember.

What happens when we put the image of smallness behind us and instead claim our *bigness*? Will big bears who stalk us in the night run away? Maybe. What is more important is that we *rise* to our fullest capabilities and become all that we are. Instead of shrinking and disappearing, we expand and appear. When we imagine ourselves as whole instead of fractured, deep rather than shallow, able versus disabled, brimming instead of insufficient, and big versus small, we are on the way to creating a new metaphor for healthy self-care.

Relationships as Metaphor

The care and nurturing of relationships might well be the most challenging work of our lives, but we need positive imagery to support that work. We can imagine our relationships like a building: *built* upon a *foundation* of respect, with the *framework* of honesty and communication, *solid* upon the *footings* of trust and love. If our relationships are not *constructed* with such *strength,* they become *shaky* and likely will *collapse.*

Relationships can also be described in the images of a journey: *So far, we have covered much ground along our path* together. In order for us to *see clearly* the *obstacles that stand in our way* and not *go around them,* we must *progress* by *going into them further.*

Additionally, relationships can be described as having qualities associated with the realm of the subconscious. The negative aspects of unhealthy relationships can be described within the metaphor of a nightmare—dreams of darkness that frighten and dismay. The nightmare—a terrifying account in which the dreamer feels the emotions of helplessness, extreme anxiety, or sorrow—describes the negative aspects of too many relationships. Conversely, a relationship that is a "dream" is a metaphor that suggests something of almost unimaginable beauty, in which the dreamer moves with ease and joy. Compare the following two possibilities:

Nightmare	Dream
Closed	Open
Running	Flying
Suffocating	Breathing
Rigid	Flexible
Ugly Monsters	Attractive beauty
Explosive	Great Chemistry
Argue	Dialogue
Mean	Playful
Ill	Healthy
Fear	Love
Mistrust	Trust

Buried	Floating
Black and White	Colorful
Dark	Light

It is clear to each of us which kind of relationship we would enjoy. If we are trapped in the unhealthy and dangerous "nightmare" relationship, the opposite possibility is a healthy and necessary alternative.

Metaphors of Work

Metaphors know no bounds, because the world upon which we sail is a metaphor. Metaphors are everywhere, applied to all aspects of life, and often shape life-action around them. It seems clear that the world of work is a fast-paced, often a fever-pitched, race against the competition that is right on your tail. Consider the positive imagery required for a successful car race:

Speed	Cheering audience
Control	Turning the corner
Power	Staying on track
Performance	Ramping up
Wheels are turning	First out of the gate

Now consider the negative imagery involved in an unsuccessful car race:

Burned out	Grind it out
Fired	Feeling rusty
Exhaust(ed)	Running out of gas
Pits	Broken down
Lug	Out of the race
Red Flag	Cracked up
Backfire	

If your perception of your work is that it has become a "constant grind" that seems like "an endless race", then you can see how such imagery has been applied to your world of work. Work has become the metaphor of a car race. Is it any wonder that there are books on achieving life-balance when speed (and winning) is the number one goal in life? It is time for a new image.

26

Work as Art

Ponder the following images:

Skillful	Picturesque	Monumental
Tasteful	Sculpturesque	Playful
Beautiful	Creative	Meaningful
Natural	Legacy	Well-arranged
Ingenious	Well-grouped	Well-composed
Aesthetic	Pleasing	Symbolic

Definitions of Work:

"A treating of the commonplace with the feeling of the sublime" (Millet)
"The conveyance of spirit by means of matter" (Salvador de Madariaga)
"Knowledge made efficient by skill" (Genung)
"The expression of one soul talking to another" (Ruskin)
"An instant arrested in eternity" (James Huneker)
"A handicraft in flower" (George Iles)
"Science in the flesh" (Jean Cocteau)
"Life upon a larger scale" (E. B.Browning)
"Nature made by Man to Man the interpreter of God" (Owen Merideth)
"A shadow of the divine perfection" (Michelangelo)
"Life seen through a temperament" (Zola)
"A form of catharsis" (Dorothy Parker)

If we can begin to imagine the metaphor of our work as our art, we can begin a process of changing how we work. We can approach each product development as an inspiration of the Divine, communicating through the "flesh" of the artist, spirit into matter. If that became the norm, we could be proud of all that we create. Our art might become a lasting legacy, so when future generations gazed upon our work, we could feel a sense of accomplishment and pride in how we contributed—how we made a difference.

Understanding through Story

Stories are sacred. Whether it is "another" story of how Uncle Walter was going to make a million dollars, why Aunt Marian was called Aunt Mooie, or even the story of America's public school desegregation—every story has something to teach us. A tradition as ancient as humanity itself, the power of story telling is that it gets right to the core of our being. A natural form of coherence, a story creates images in the mind while simultaneously touching the emotions of the heart, thus unifying heart and mind in the common pursuit of learning.

Stories also have a way of breaking down the walls of resistance. I had a mentor who inevitably responded to an issue or challenge I was facing with, "This reminds me of a story . . ." By the time he was finished, I had gotten the point. Rarely did he ever tell me what to do or give advice. Instead, he let the story teach me what I needed to know and what could be done to meet the challenge. While pondering the meaning within the story, any resistance to change that I may have felt was melted away by the light of understanding.

I recently attended a National Storytellers Festival in Jonesborough, Tennessee—an annual event that began over 25 years ago. Thousands of people gather each autumn in Tennessee's oldest town to hear storytellers paint word pictures with nostalgia and humor, to recall everyday feelings and uncommon events of the good life. For two days, I sat in white, circus-like tents along with hundreds of others, as each of us experienced the meaning of a "full heart," an inspired mind, and souls that danced with laughter. From the "Jack" tales of the Tennessee mountains to the ghost tales of master-teller Kathryn Wyndam, every cell of my body seemed to vibrate with the beautifully crafted words of each story.

Each of us has a story. It is a sacred story because it is the story of our journey. It has humor, pain, bliss, and despair throughout, with a collection of characters who enter in and out of the ongoing plot at will. Our story shapes us and we shape it. Formless, yet not without structure, in retrospect, everything in our stories has meaning and purpose. The following two stories are not uncommon, yet they are unique. Both characters, in their own way, have learned something about life-balance through the wisdom of experience.

Harold Green

Harold Green is a local California character who lives a life of integrity and generous spirit, and who doesn't know the meaning of retirement. Still working five days a week for an hourly wage to supplement his limited income, Mr. Green is an 80-year-old handyman who specializes in repairing Eichler homes, a design native to northern California. Driving a 1973 Honda (which cost $50), he recently paid a visit to my good friend Laura's home, to give her an estimate for repairing the tracks of some sliding closet doors. Laura had already received an estimate for $1600 to replace the doors, which she could not even consider because of her own budget limitations. Mr. Green assured her that it would only take two hours to return the tracks and doors to their original condition.

Climbing up and down his rickety ladder served as a perfect backdrop for Laura and Mr. Green to exchange life stories including those of children and grandchildren. When finished with both the stories and the closet doors, Mr. Green informed Laura that his fee was $20 per hour, for a total of $40. Laura protested, since $100 per hour was more the norm for this area of California. Believing his wage to be fair, Mr. Green took her check, put his rickety ladder in his equally rickety car, and happily entered rush-hour traffic to return home. This man of energy and commitment left Laura's home with far more than closet doors that worked. He left in her heart the legacy of his personal story as well as his generous spirit.

The Handkerchief

Two years had passed since Sara Pratt's father died. "Two years!" she thought, as she arranged the fresh Iris just the way he had always done. Oh, how she missed him. His laugh, his willingness to listen. He was always there for her—a marvelous friend. The memory of her father brought tears to Sara's eyes, and she put down the pruning shears to replace them with a handful of tissue. Wiping her eyes, she—almost ceremoniously— walked toward the large dresser in her bedroom. She must have made this ritual trek a thousand times over the past two years; it was her way of remembering her father. Reaching for the top left drawer, she slowly pulled it open and watched as its contents were revealed. On the left was the ring her mother had given her when she was sixteen. It had been her grandmother's engagement ring, worn thin by the years and now too fragile to wear. It glistened in the morning light and highlighted more memories of days gone by. Although she had loved her mother, she didn't miss the tension that always seemed to have surrounded their relationship. Perhaps her mother was threatened by Sara's relationship with her father. He always treated her as "his little girl." "Mother couldn't handle that," she thought. "Everyone wanted his attention. I just happened to be the one who received it."

James L. Pratt had been a man the world would refer to as "successful." He loved his work and he lived life with passion and purpose. Starting his own business at the age of 19, he had a way of knowing the needs of humanity before they became evident to the rest of the world. Inventor, artist, and creator of "something out of nothing," James was successful at everything he did. He moved as if in sync with the Universe, flowing from one phase to the next. Although he never sought to make money, money seemed to make its way to him. Untouched by material gain, he lived a simple, yet elegant lifestyle.

Sara reached for the object she kept hidden in the back of the drawer. It was a curious memento of her father—not one others would cherish. But she thought it was so like him. It was a fine, elegant, thread of seamless weave that represented his very life. Perhaps from China, the object blended the fabric of East with West, a perfect reminder of her father, whose life knew no bounds. Moving aside a small card that covered and protected her reminder, she lifted a white handkerchief and lifted it toward her as if it were a small dove. Ceremoniously raising it to her nose, she drew in a deep breath, inhaling the reminiscent scent of her father. The fragrance of the man she so admired and loved still remained intact within this piece of fabric that had become, for her, a sacred object.

Carefully folding the handkerchief and placing it on top of the dresser, Sara rearranged the family pictures as a tear rolled down her cheek. Most prominent in the picture collection was a photo of Sara and her father, taken when she was only seven years old. He held her in his arms as the two laughed and posed for a shot that would become a lasting centerpiece in her collection of memories. Yet the fragrance of the handkerchief was the most important reminder of the best friend who was now gone.

Sara's ritual was something she shared with no one. Performed in the privacy of her bedroom, she would have been embarrassed if others knew of her devotional act. Her mother had "let her father go" long before her own death, and she counseled Sara to do the same. Unwilling or unable, Sara did not let go, but continued to invoke his memory through the lasting fragrance of Bay Rum cologne.

The ringing of the doorbell interrupted the silence of her private ritual. Sara left the bedroom, quickly closing the door behind her. The cleaning service had arrived for their weekly task, and Sara decided to leave the house so as not to interfere with their work. Returning home several hours later with her two children, the remainder of Sara's day was filled with family activities. It was not until bedtime that she returned to her freshly cleaned bedroom. Noticing that the family pictures had been rearranged by the cleaning service, she returned them back to their familiar positions. "I like things to stay the same," she thought. "If only they could," she sighed as she glanced at the photograph of her father.

Opening the drawer for just one comforting breath of her father's scent, she lifted the protective card that guarded the handkerchief from any curious intruder. Panic suddenly overcame her and her heart pounded furiously. The handkerchief was not there. Frantically she searched the drawer, removing the contents in case she had carelessly misplaced it. "Where could it be?!" she cried aloud. "What could have happened?" Sara continued her frantic search, scrutinizing every corner of the bedroom. Hoping that the handkerchief might have fallen behind it, she moved the dresser away from the wall. But her effort was fruitless.

Falling back upon her bed, she began to cry deep tears. Fear overcame her as she was forced to accept that the last remnant of her father was gone forever. Reaching for the pile of clean towels on her bed, she instead lifted a clean, pressed handkerchief to her swollen eyes. At that moment she realized what had happened: when she abruptly walked out of the room to answer the ringing doorbell, she had foolishly left her father's handkerchief on top of the dresser. It had simply become a part of the weekly laundry, with a detergent scent like any other newly-washed family fabric.

The only remaining memento of Sara's father was gone forever. She could hear her deceased mother's lingering words: "Sara, you *have* to let him go."

LESSONS AS GUIDES

Golf does not build character—it exposes it!

My father's greatest contribution to my development was teaching me the game of golf at a very young age. As an eight-year-old, I spent hours slugging around the little nine-hole course to which he belonged. I learned the difference between a driver, a brassie, and a spoon, as well as how to "keep

31

my head down" as I chopped away with my wooden-shafted clubs. Getting the ball to the hole afforded me many options at the age of eight: teeing up in the fairway; throwing the ball by hand from the sand trap; defining a "gimmee" as anything under six feet from the hole. The Mulligan (taking a second shot off the first tee), was another natural and "most acceptable" deviation from the rules.

When I was 11, my boyhood friend Billy Madison and I each entered the Junior Championship, in which players up to the age of 18 were eligible. No longer were we able to play according to our boyhood rules; *now* we had to play in accordance with championship guidelines. After nine holes, Billy and I were tied at 48. The second nine holes would prove who had worked the hardest—or had the best luck. It was not a competition against all others in the field so much as it was one between the two boys from Green Street. Reaching the last hole, we were still tied at 90, and we each finished the round with a 95—rather remarkable for an 11- and thirteen-year-old. However, since Billy's handicap was less than mine, he had to concede a stroke. I won by that one stroke—not only our "private" match but, as it turned out, the championship as well. That taught me a life lesson—*you can play according to the rules and still win.*

Many years later, a golf professional taught me another essential life-lesson when he said, "How you do anything is how you do everything! How you play golf is how you will live your life." I pondered these wise words from that 5'3" mystic, and they seemed to make a lot of sense. But it was not until I saw him drive a ball 300 yards from a kneeling position that those words had real credibility. I figured, "He must have spent a lot of time on his knees and anyone with that devotion must know what he is talking about."

Today, I continue to love the game of golf and play by its rules, but I have always (without guilt) *used a Mulligan.* It was not until my father's funeral recently that I finally learned from him, post-mortem, perhaps the final lesson in the game of golf—and life. When friends were invited to speak at his memorial service, his golf partner rose to his feet. "As his golf partner for the past 30 years, there is one defining aspect of character that I will remember most about Bob Patnaude," said the aged golfer. "He never took a Mulligan." I sat stunned at this public pronouncement about this man with whom I had played golf countless times. I was with him at Pebble Beach when he birdied the famous seventh hole, and for years I watched him characteristically lift his left foot and bite his lip with each shot. How had I *not* known that this man would not take the "free" shot that almost every golfer in the world has come to believe is his or her right? I felt immense admiration for this small businessman, who had suddenly become larger than life.

I thank my father for teaching me the game of golf with all of its life-lessons. And his final lesson of wisdom—NO MULLIGANS!

In my work of helping to develop authentic leaders over the years, I have applied this golf wisdom to life and leadership:

- If we cheat on our score, we will cheat on our taxes.
- If we are always buying the newest equipment in an effort to improve our game, we will surround ourselves with material things to improve our lives.
- If we lose our concentration after one triple bogey, we will not be able to handle the hard times.
- If we do not allow faster players to "play through," we will lack the same courtesy skills in relationships.
- If we step in the lie of our competition, we will not play fair in any contest.
- If we lift our head before we actually hit the ball, we will be more interested in the outcome than process.
- If we lose sight of the beauty of the setting and view the course only as something to conquer, we will miss the beauty of each day.

Such simple wisdom comes from pondering the lessons learned from life-experience. When we learn to listen with the eyes of the heart and the ears of the mind, and then ponder the meaning of the experience, we will discover the lessons that come to us as our guides. Sometimes deeply hidden, often as exposed as sitting on a ledge, these lessons become travel partners along our path. Some of the lessons I have learned:

- Only attempt to change another when you are finished with changing yourself.
- Telling the truth is easiest because you do not ever have to try and remember what you've said.

⊠ Giving is richer than getting.

⊠ Everything is connected.

⊠ Live with questions.

⊠ Play without a reason.

⊠ Life is to be lived in the fullest—now.

⊠ SACRED SPIRIT — ENERGY ECOLOGY

*We all have a specific purpose; we all have something for which each of us,
and each of us alone, is responsible.* —NAOMI STEPHANI

Whatever the roots of our religious backgrounds, there is a common ground in Spirit as eternal spark. Spirit is the source of the ignition of the "big explosion" that brought all the possibilities of the dream into play. It is the energy that moves us from lethargy to action, immobility to meaning. It is the power behind legacy; the push behind the pull.

As Erotic Intelligence awakens us from our sleep and the Mystical Mind allows us time to ponder wisdom, it is the energy of Sacred Spirit that moves us into action. Sacred Spirit is a transformative power that can turn average into excellence. It can move us from the limited realm of performance to the vast world of understanding. Although efficiency appears to reign supreme in the business world, love is the most potent force that can transform the bottom-line toward higher good. It is only in the realm of Spirit that misery can become mastery, monks can become mystics and martyrs can become mentors.

Perhaps a more universal understanding of Spirit allows us to see it as pure energy, for without such energy, beginnings do not occur; it is the essential resource for stimulating life. In the birth of every child, the world begins again. Within the romance of any relationship, energy is the source of passion and embrace. Within an organization that reflects the energy of good values and a shared vision, there are no limitations. And within the community of neighborhood or nation, energy is the creative force that can bring about wholeness or destruction. But although energy cannot permanently cease-and-desist, it is important to realize that it ebbs and flows—it *can* be depleted or renewed. And if serious depletion occurs, functioning is impaired.

Depletion

There was a famous monastery that had fallen on very hard times. Formerly, its many buildings were filled with young monks and its big church resounded with the singing of the chants. But now it was deserted. People no longer came there to be nourished by prayer. A handful of old monks shuffled through the cloisters and praised their God with heavy hearts.

On the edge of the monastery woods, an old rabbi had built a little hut. He would come there from time to time to fast and pray. No one ever spoke to him, but whenever he appeared, the word would be passed from monk to monk: "The rabbi walks in the woods. The rabbi walks in the woods." And, for as long as he was there, the monks would feel sustained by his prayerful presence.

One day the abbot decided to visit the rabbi and to open his heart to him. After the morning Eucharist, he set out through the woods. As he approached, the abbot found the rabbi standing in the doorway of the hut, his arms outstretched in welcome. It was as though he had been waiting there for some time. The two embraced like long-lost brothers. Then they stepped back and just stood there, smiling at one another with smiles their faces could hardly contain.

After a while, the rabbi motioned the abbot to enter. In the middle of the hut was a wooden table with the Scripture open on it. They sat together at the table in the presence of the Word. Then the rabbi began to cry. The abbot could not contain himself. He covered his face with his hands and he too began to cry. For the first time in his life, he cried his heart out. The two men sat there like lost children, filling the hut with their sobs and wetting the Word with their tears.

After the tears had ceased to flow and all was quiet again, the rabbi raised his head. "You and your brothers are serving God with heavy hearts," he said. "You have come to ask a teaching of me. I will give you a teaching, but you can only repeat it once. After that, no one must ever say it aloud again."

The rabbi gazed at the abbot and said, "The Messiah is among you." He said nothing more.

The abbot left without a word and without ever looking back.

The next morning, the abbot called his monks together in the chapter room. He told them he had received a teaching from "the rabbi who walks in the woods" and that this teaching was never again to be spoken aloud. Then he gazed at each of his brothers and said, "The rabbi said that one of us is the Messiah."

The monks were startled by this teaching. "What could it possibly mean?" they asked themselves. "Is Brother John the Messiah? Or Father Matthew? Or Brother

Thomas? Am I the Messiah? What could this mean?" They were all deeply puzzled by the rabbi's teaching. But no one ever mentioned it again.

As time went by, the monks began to treat one another with a very special reverence. There was a gentle, wholehearted, human quality about them now, that was hard to describe but easy to notice. They lived with one another as men who had finally found something. But they prayed the Scriptures together as men who were always looking for something. Occasional visitors found themselves deeply moved by the life of these monks. Before long, people were coming from far and wide to be nourished by the prayer life of the monks, and young men were asking, once again, to live with the monks for a lifetime.

In those days, the rabbi no longer walked in the woods. His hut had fallen into ruins, but somehow or other, the old monks who had taken his teaching to heart still felt sustained by his prayerful presence . . . They still felt sustained by his prayerful presence.

The Rabbi's Gift, an untold story by FRANCIS DORFF, O. PRAEM originally published by *The Catholic World*

Our Erotic Intelligence and Mystical Minds alert us when depletion occurs. We know and experience the loss of energy, like the air leaking slowly out of a balloon. We can feel the effort it takes to move our tired bodies, taste the sourness of daily routine, see the immobility of the human spirit, smell the disease of lacking a life-purpose and hear the gripe of bitterness. Our brains lack creative drive and our hearts become heavy with sorrow without the life-giving energy of Spirit.

The monastic community in the story above lost its energy because it had depleted the Spirit that was the source of its purpose and passion. It was only when the monks rediscovered the reverence and trust in meaningful relationship that they again felt the rush of Divine breath that became the praise of their renewed heart songs.

Since life can be described as energy in process, depletion occurs in all aspects of life. Like a sailboat going "into irons" without the energy of the wind to move it forward, all relationships can experience the same inert prison. Often, when the energy of passion is gone, the only remnants are multiple attachments or mutual dependencies.

It was in the fifteenth year of my 18-year marriage that I knew my soul was dying. I began to feel lifeless and discouraged, and even lacked desire for my work which, until then, had always been my greatest love and an art form. My relationship with my daughters was also suffering, as absence from the home became my avenue for survival. I "buried" myself in my work and in the sorrow for the pain all of us were feeling. It became clear that I had to make a dramatic change in order to save my relationship with my children, as well as the health of my soul. Twelve years later, I live with the responsibility for failing to keep a promise that I always believed in and intended to uphold, yet I again delight in the renewed energy of Spirit that flows through me.

The same Spirit that flows through us individually flows through groups and organizations which can also experience the depletion of this energy. Many corporations can make huge profits, and at the same time, hemorrhage spiritually. Some years ago, in response to an inquiry about our leadership programs, I walked into the shiny towers of an internationally known company. Although I was standing in a cavernous lobby surrounded by new, sparkling glass, I felt an interior heaviness. As my Erotic Intelligence gathered data that seemed to conflict with the outer image the company was attempting to project, I was escorted to the meeting.

Intrigued by my proposal about leadership development, the company contracted us to begin a pilot leadership program. Even though I agreed, I still felt my Spirit resist moving ahead. Four months later, after experiencing too many occasions of mistrust, lies, and internal power games, I terminated our relationship. Although it meant the loss of considerable work and income for my company, it was clearly the best decision *not* to become part of a vortex of such negative energy. Additional information eventually confirmed that what we had experienced was considered to be the normal operating style for this company. It was the way the CEO operated and, consequently, it became the pattern of behavior for the entire corporation. Although they continue to be profitable, today, the trust factor appears to be minimal and their turnover rate is very high. Why?

When any of us live or work in an environment that embraces values that are in conflict with our personal values, our souls will begin a process of interior disturbance in order to remove us from that which threatens our spiritual health. Despite monetary security or reward, if we stay on a path that disconnects us from our spiritual energy, we begin the process of slow death, which continues unless something begins to change.

Change — The Magic of Alchemy

Energy is always moving and changing, for change is the way of the Universe. According to the ancient Greek philosopher Heraclitus, "the *only* constant is change." Change is so much a natural way of life that its flow results in momentous and seemingly unpredictable shifts. Long periods of chaos and disorder can shift abruptly, evolving into a stage of stability and predictability. Likewise, after long periods of routine and regularity, change again leads to chaos and creative disorder.

The alchemist's lifelong pursuit was to change lead into gold. Modern-day alchemists are silicon engineers who have learned a faster way to wealth through the process of changing sand into microprocessors, worth much more than gold itself. In the land of microprocessors (Silicon Valley, California), companies thrive or die because of change.

Someone once said wisely, "Those who resist change die, those who tolerate change survive, but those who embrace change, thrive." In this realm of constant change, it is imperative to learn how to reformulate the way we think. Consciousness cannot be institutionalized or routinized. Like the pathway of a great river, consciousness must be "in process," for without movement, it becomes stagnant.

The path of natural change-process has change-points that punctuate three distinct growth phases: forming, norming and performing. Phase One, the *formative* phase, is the period of exploration and experiment, as one begins to pull things together to shape something new. Change occurs and pulls the process into Phase Two, the *normative* phase, when the random process ceases and norms become an orderly and predictable pattern. In order for growth to continue however, another change-point must occur. This in turn produces Phase Three, the *performing* phase, which is a reconfiguration of the *normative* phase and includes new energy and ideas, often elements previously rejected in the normative phase. What pulls an existing stage into the new form is a dramatic change-event at the culmination of the growth phase. If the growth cycle becomes complete, the energetic stage of *transforming* occurs, which returns the cycle to Phase One, yet at a much higher level. While each stage is necessary for evolution to the highest form, it is not always easy, expedient, or painless.

Examples

Our planet is still in the process of following its own growth cycle. When our solar system began four-and-a-half billion years ago, the planet Earth was a complex group of molecules in chaos. The natural entrepreneurial spirit of life sought a multitude of ways to assemble repeatable patterns in order to sustain continued growth; most failed. Yet after about one billion years of experimentation the cell emerged as a unit, with its own regulatory systems for internal ingestion, membrane protection, and DNA code—all to determine a blueprint for future potential. Then change happened.

Phase Two occurred when the cell was able to manufacture a likeness of itself within an established pattern that could allow repetition. What began next was an unprecedented cycle of reproduction that dominated the planet for the next one billion years, as the original pattern extended itself, and even modified and improved upon the original prototype.

If survival were the only goal of this new cellular creation, the life-cycle would have ended here. Ancestors of this nucleated cell can still be found today in the deep recesses of ocean canyons or buried deep in the polar ice caps. But in the quest for excellence and full potential, the second dramatic change-point occurred and the Phase Three phenomena began to reveal one of nature's most important secrets: cells began to share differences rather than build upon similarities. In other words, A combined with B to create hybrid C—a universal law of nature. This occurred only by opening up the constrictive nature locked within each individual cell, and combining that nature with that of the uniquely different neighboring cell. The transformation of our planet began when these combinations became complex organisms that eventually evolved into multi-cellular plant life.

As we can see,

> nature does not operate in a logical, regular, and predictable progression, but is engaged in a dynamic creative process, bringing into being what never before existed. Nature follows a very special pattern. She weaves in and out of ordering and reordering, encountering change-points along the way. The phenomena that are often labeled 'disorder' and 'randomness' actually operate to provide necessary opportunities to develop deeper, broader, and more complex connections. People, ideas, and things connect both internally and with the external environment as the three phases of creative growth and change progress. This allows nature—including us—to make giant, unpredictable leaps in evolution and creativity. New species appear! Unique cells, plants, animals and varied forms of organized life emerge. Constant change hallmarks our planet—and our lives.

—GEORGE LAND, *Breakpoint and Beyond*

Flowing *with* change—as opposed to against it—is a key to living simultaneously.

Relationships and Change

Any love relationship can move through all three stages of the change-cycle and can be tracked through the interesting phraseology we have created to describe this process: in *Forming*, we *"fall* in love;" in *Norming*, we "go *steady.*" Then, after some period of disillusionment, we effect change-points through *"breaking up."* If they are willing to move into *Performing*, partners must renew their commitment and begin the transformation work necessary for establishing a long-lasting relationship—a relationship that will require multiple re-inventions in order to thrive.

In relationships, the first stage of forming is defined as the period of romance, when all brain functions cease and Erotic Intelligence is captain of the star-struck ship. It is a stage of rapid change in which our world seems to be transforming at lightning speed, and phrases like "falling in love" best describe our condition. Since Eros is the power that attracts us to that which we believe will complete us, the blood in our veins flows with the speed of Mercury, and the heart of Aphrodite beats as we *fall* into the abyss toward wholeness.

I remember experiencing such heart-pounding palpitations in the first grade, when I was in love with Michele Drew. Although she did not know it, this one-sided love affair was to become a monumental memory in my developing saga of romance. After watching this adorable brunette from afar, I made my first move in the basement cafeteria of our neighborhood school. As I rounded the corner after paying the cashier 20 cents for mashed potatoes, canned peas, and chicken breast, I saw her SITTING ALONE! This was my big chance to have her notice me. Catching my foot underneath the leg of a folding chair, I *did* make my way toward her, only . . . it was through the air. Falling flat on the floor with my face landing in my lunch plate, I lifted my head, now partially covered with potatoes and peas, to see Michelle giggling at the sight of this love-struck puppy at her feet. I had achieved my goal: she *did* notice me. Although that first encounter did not go as planned, we did end up "going steady" in the eighth grade, thus completing Stages One and Two of this—my first experience of romantic love.

Stage Two, "going steady," is exactly that—creating a wonderful and mutually reinforcing pattern that steadily provides routine and order for love to flourish. This is the period of understanding each other's anomalies, needs, and desires, and responding appropriately. Replacing toothpaste caps, choosing who has which side of the bed, the strategic place-ment of wet towels, and where you leave your shoes, are all most impor-tant elements in understanding the meaning of "steady." Knowing how much time one requires at the airport before takeoff, who pays the bills and balances the checkbook, and who does "what" with the toilet seat, are all quality indicators when asked, "How's it going?" This is the period for dis-covering the meaning of words like rhythm, synchronicity, compassion, and intimacy. If those gems do not become woven into the fabric of the relationship, *steady* becomes a thing of the past and *rocky* emerges as the state of the union.

Couples have an important choice as the second change-point emerges. One choice is to continue the relationship, as-is, and risk its ultimate death as it spirals downward. Another choice is to end the relationship and each participant goes out, eventually to begin Phase One with someone else. Or the couple can choose to work at reinventing of the existing relationship, deleting negative behaviors and establishing new rules in order to breathe new life back into the partnership. It is here that Phase Three emerges and demands, not a remake of the old, but something creative and new, if the relationship is to flourish.

As a season ticket-holder for Stanford University Football, I have the privilege of sitting next to a married couple who have held season tickets for 53 years. They have watched countless great athletes mature in their skills before going on to become professional players. Jim Plunkett, John Elway, James Lofton, John Brodie, Frankie Albert, Bob Matthias, and Gene Washington are just a sampling of this couple's historical football record. But even more wonderful is the fact that Ressa and Marvin have been married for 56 years. Present on every game day, this marvelous twosome exhibits the same fan-like enthusiasm for each other as they do for the players. Holding hands while exchanging play-by-play comments, they appear to be the epitome of relationship transformation and ongoing re-invention. Having experienced so many different Stanford football teams, most likely, they have also re-engineered their own team almost as many times.

The three phases of the natural life-change cycle constitute an im-portant lens through which we can view life. It is a process that gives us some very wise guidelines for creating a dynamic life, whether personal or organizational:

❈ Create what has never existed before: do not depend just on improvements to what already exists

❈ Make deep and powerful interdependent connections with one another, not to exclude people based on differences or separate functions

❈ "Be *pulled* to a new kind of future, not *pushed* by the past."
(GEORGE LAND and BETH JARMON, *Breakpoint and Beyond*)

All of us find ourselves—at some time, somewhere—in the downward spiral of depletion. "Exhausted," "spent," "worn-out," "burned out," "run-down," "done," or "wasted" are just some of the expressions we use to describe this condition of emptiness. Although the wisdom of our bodies suggests removal from a negative routine and the necessity of a long and deep rest, depletion is not only a condition of the physical self. Depletion occurs throughout our entire system of mind, body, and Spirit, and in our desire for rebirth, the unified self cries out for change and the fresh air of renewal.

Renewal

The fresh air of renewal blows through stagnation like a sea breeze through tired urban air. It is as essential in everyone's work as it is in every relationship. The rediscovery of passion and meaning reminds us of what originally attracted us to our heart's focus and then whispers the encouragement to begin again.

Sometimes, renewal comes from recognizing that the lure of conventional boxes is like a siren calling us to its suffocating grasp. Returning to what is safe, because it is what we know, is not always the best path as it limits our spirit to "what was" rather than "what can be." Such box-like thinking can be a negative reminder of what we do not want and what we do not deserve and may recommit us to continue onward along our path of meaning and purpose. Movement and change is the way of the Universe and the way in which we reinvent ourselves many times over.

The Universe just reminded me of this lesson, for as I write these words I am reinventing what I wrote yesterday. The entire work of yesterday morning was lost due to a "glitch" in the process of saving the material. At first I panicked, making various attempts to retrieve "what was," rather than believing that I could recreate the ideas; I followed a predictable path of anxiety rather than calling upon Sacred Spirit for renewing the thoughts. I felt discouraged and tired. Then an e-mail message arrived from my daughter Laura, who is studying in Europe:

Dear Daddy:

I just wanted to say how much I am thinking of you and how much you are in my heart. I talk about you all the time to my friends, and I am so fortunate to have you as my father. You are such a mentor to me even though I am halfway around the world. I can feel such a connection with you from here even though we don't talk as much as we do when I am at school in the States. I look forward to the day we work together so I can learn and grow with you and from you. I love you so much. Thank you for being my Daddy.

Heartened, tearful, and with spirit lifted, I walked to the mailbox. Among the hoard of mail (that none of us ever seem to request), was a card from my daughter Julie. It read:

Hi Dad:

I just want to write a quick note to say thank you for being an amazing Dad. You give so abundantly and I thank you so much. I want to hug you daily. I love you.

How could one *not* be touched by such a synchronistic outreach of love? Emboldened and renewed, I began to write again. From where does this Spirit come? What is the source of this unlimited energy that creates and transforms? Is it an energy that comes from outside to our weary selves like a healing balm, or is it a power that lives within each one of us and needs only the spark of love to ignite?

Author and teacher Carolyn Myss tells the moving story of a Native American man who was injured in war. Crippled and relegated to a wheelchair for the rest of his life, he returned home to his tribe. The tribal elders, unwilling to accept the limitation of physical immobility, wheeled him to a nearby lake, lifted him out of his chair, threw him into the water and said, "Call upon your Spirit to renew your body and save your life." The paralyzed body of the young soldier began to sink to the bottom of the lake. Unable to move his arms or legs, his only choice was to follow the wisdom of his elders so he called upon Spirit for the renewal of his body. As if he were being born anew from his mother's womb, the young man's body began to feel regeneration emerge and strength return to his lifeless limbs. Able to move his arms and legs enough to swim, he broke through the water's surface and was pulled to safety by the expectant elders. Within time, his body recovered fully, and today he walks without assistance.

Twelve years ago, I began my work in the realm of Spirit and Business. Although today there are more books and conferences on the subject than I would ever have imagined then (1988), I often felt like a lone voice "crying in the wilderness." When asked how I would *bring* Spirit to the workplace, I was very clear that my work was not about *bringing* anything; that would be presumptuous and arrogant. Instead, I grew to understand my purpose as calling forth the Spirit that already resides within any organization. Though almost buried sometimes or very often murky, Spirit *is* present because it resides within the soul of every worker. Like the great teacher who "draws out" rather than "fills up" the student's mind, my work would not be a process of imposing energy from the outside/in; in contrast, it would become a process that led from the inside/out.

Inside / Out

If we observe the life-cycle of a seed we observe the natural process for living. Within the seed's genetic code is the potential for fullness and fruit, but the process of change and transformation that occurs is its own genius. Beginning with a hard exterior, it is planted to begin a process of softening and change. Roots begin to grow downward as it builds its foundational system for support and nourishment. Delicate shoots grow upward as it seeks the light that will become its source of energy and constant renewal. Eventually, it will produce a flower or seed for furthering its species in a natural way of proliferation. The seed participates in an ancient ritual with the earth—a sacred dance toward completion through the process of birth, death, and rebirth.

One of the most powerful women I know is my friend and guide, Angeles Arrien, an author, teacher, and mystic. I have watched Angie teach for seven consecutive days without experiencing any noticeable signs of depletion. She is forever present and fully engaged, seemingly drawing energy from an overflowing well within. When I asked her how she did it, she revealed one of her secrets: she spends two hours each day in nature. Remaining silent, she works in her gardens or just spends her time contemplating the mystery and beauty of what lives around her. Drawing from the earth energy of Gaia, her spirit is renewed for meeting the challenging demands of her daily schedule.

When I am not on a training floor, I have the advantage of working from my home office. After some bouts of concentrated focus, I go into my yard to pull weeds or trim roses. My neighbors often wonder if I have a "real" job, since I frequently communicate with those who pass by and observe my gardens or my sleeping dog. As if I've had a power nap, I experience the renewal of my energy and am ready to return to my work.

In *Love for Space* (Circle Two), I will describe a project now in the early stages of development, The Spiritual Village. The dream includes a vineyard as well as orchards that will surround this center, where depleted souls not only can experience the renewal that comes through creative programs, but also will have the opportunity, each day, to "work the land." Confident that Gaia will teach as much as the seminars we offer, the renewal that participants will seek just might be found at the end of a hoe.

The renewal that comes from the inside/out might be described as "deep pleasure." In contrast to the death-dealing depletion, deep pleasure is the way of autonomy, self-mastery, wise choices, awakened senses, inner power, community, humility, generosity, and gratitude. It becomes the pathway for bliss and the way of life lived simultaneously. The deep pleasure of renewal is so powerful that it can transform our zeal for performance into a capacity for understanding: instead of efficiency, our priority becomes compassion; instead of the bottom line, our goal is the highest good.

For example, in today's modern society of efficiency, success is measured by what we produce. Quotas, bottom-lines, and "raising the bar" are all ways in which we define success. I would like to suggest the opposite, and say that we are not measured by *what* we produce, but rather *how* we produce and *why* we produce. If we were to compare a family that has 12 children who are unloved and undernourished with a family that has two children who are honored and loved, there would be no contest. "Big" or "more" is not always better. Why, then, are we so enamored with the measure of production? Perhaps it is because we are a people more in need of spiritual renewal than we are in need of accumulated matter. We Americans especially need to pay attention to the fact that our fascination with production and our addiction to consumption may be the death knell for our weary planet, which is currently seeking its own form of renewal.

45

Good News, Great News—The Triumph of Spirit

What happens when the renewing power of Sacred Spirit is on the loose? Anything is possible. Consider the story of company owner Bob Thompson who sold his Michigan road-building firm for $422 million. Having started his business 40 years ago from his basement office on a mere $3500, Thompson's net profit could have put him in the same league as Silicon Valley superstars or top sports figures. But Thompson had another idea, so he called his employees together and told them that he had good news. The Ireland-based company buying his company was known for *not* breaking up companies, so they would keep all their jobs. And then, after delivering this good news, he had some *great* news: he would be sharing $128 million among his 550 employees, making more than 80 devoted workers millionaires. "They deserve it," he said. "People work hard for us—14-hour days, six-day weeks, 99-degree heat, and 300-degree asphalt. Some people make a lot of money in the stock market, but we're dependent on people, so it just would not be fair *not* to do it."

As the sale became final, hourly workers, most of whom already had pensions, received $2000 for each year of service, and some checks exceeded annual salaries. Salaried workers who did not have pensions were given checks or annuity certificates that ranged from $1 million to $2 million apiece. Thompson even included some retirees and widows in his plan. And as if that were not enough, he also paid all the taxes on their gifts which amounted to another $25 million.

The story of French journalist Jean-Dominique Bauby is another testimony to the power of the indominable nature of Spirit. A career journalist whose wit, flair and *savoir-vivre* became his personal trademark, he experienced his fast-paced life come to an abrupt end on December 8, 1995, when he suffered a paralyzing stroke. Completely dependent upon medical machinery for all of his bodily functions, the only part of Bauby that remained unscathed by this trauma was the quality of his brain and the determination of his Spirit. Discovering that his left eyelid was the only muscle in his entire body that he was able to control, he let the nursing staff know that his winks meant he was still alive and "kicking." They responded by helping to construct an alphabet that allowed him to eventually to blink out a letter to family and friends announcing that he was not only alive but still creating as well.

What followed was a book, *The Bubble and the Butterfly*—a brilliant exposé about the "locked-in-life" with all its tedium, trials and joy. Bauby shared his frustration with not being able to do what the normal body took for granted. "I would be the happiest man in the world if I could just properly swallow the saliva that permanently invades my mouth." He described the despair of being locked in a body plagued with bedsores and flies that walked with impunity across his face. Most agonizing were his descriptions from behind the protective bubble of not being able to touch his son again or to feel the embrace of those who loved him. "Theophile, my son, is calmly sitting there, his face 20 inches from my own, and I, his father, do not have the simple right to touch his thick hair . . . to hold tight his warm, little body . . . Suddenly that fact begins killing me."

In the end, Bauby's spirit proved to be stronger than his heart. Less than 72 hours after critics hailed the completed work as a triumph and a legacy not soon to be forgotten, Jean-Dominique Bauby died. But in his death, we are only reminded of the life that lived within him and the nature of a Spirit that could not be paralyzed.

FREEDOM

Freedom is the wing upon which we can fly.

At the heart of Sacred Spirit, as evidenced in the lives of Bob Thompson, Harold Green, and Jean-Dominique Bauby, is the most fundamental element of nature—freedom. In the dream that is dreaming us, the image is one of our wholeness, our fullness, and our freedom. Freedom is at the heart of every escape attempt, whether from the chains of addiction or the prison of pretense. Freedom is the lure of Sacred Spirit, calling us out of our often-self-imposed bondage, home to the realm of our soul. Freedom is the glue of long-term relationships, the delight of self-care, and the fuel for meaningful work. Freedom is at the core of great leadership that honors the freedom of every human spirit. And freedom of choice is one of life's greatest gifts.

Living simultaneously requires the freedom to make choices. When we are free to say no or to say yes, to say something or to say nothing, we are following the pathway that leads to our soul. In contrast, when we act from the motivation of guilt or shame, when we live up to the unrealistic expectations of another or of ourselves—then we imprison the soul that wants to soar.

47

One of the often-forgotten pathways to soul flight is the freedom we have to forgive. When we condemn ourselves or others to the prison of our personal judgment, we behave inconsistently with the alchemy of change and flow. Unforgiveness is a "stuck factor" that mires us in the muck of immobility. Unresolved issues between people who live or work closely together usually create feelings of hostility and tension, and become a significant drain on our energy ecology.

Stanford University sponsored a study of 55 students who had an unresolved interpersonal issue within a close, personal relationship; the issue could not be the result of abuse or a crime. After randomization, 28 students received a six-hour training in forgiveness, based upon the cognitive-disputation techniques of Rational Emotive Therapy. The remaining 27 students served as a control group. After the training, members of the study group exhibited less anger, greater psychological well-being, they forgave the person who had hurt them, and saw forgiveness as an effective, problem-solving strategy. The scientific data suggests that negative emotions induced by past events can be released rapidly if we are provided with the appropriate tools. In the ecology of energy, in spite of often-self-defeating obsessions, the results of this study also suggest that our deepest desire is to be free of fetters so that our souls can fly.

Before venturing out into the world for "forgiveness practice," it might be a good idea to practice first, at home. What guilt and shame do we carry that we can practice letting go? What self-imposed expectations and schedules can we move from the realm of "should" into the world of "could?" When we can start forgiving ourselves for the way we act, look, and accumulate, and with patience, begin choosing the way we intend to act, look, and accumulate, we are practicing freedom. The reality is that each of us lives somewhere between special and ordinary, victim and perpetrator, predator and prey. We must give ourselves the freedom necessary to walk the path of that precarious reality, and forgive ourselves and others along the journey's way. When that happens, souls begin to soar.

Keeping Sabbath

Six days a week we wrestle with the world, wringing profit from the earth;
on the Sabbath we especially care for the seed of eternity planted in the soul.
The world has our hands, but our soul belongs to Some One Else.

— ABRAHAM HESCHEL

Spiritual traditions reserve one day for rest, renewal, re-energizing and re-birth—the seventh day of the week called Sabbath. Sabbath is a day of re-membering and forgetting: remembering what is most important and what we value most dearly, and a time to forget what demands our attention the other six days. It is a day to create sacred and open space where what and who we love can flow in and out. The seventh day is a day of peace and an armistice with what often is our struggle for existence. It is a time for mak-ing peace with ourselves and making peace with the earth that supports our exhaustive hunger, without any expectation of return. Sabbath is a holy time where the clock of midweek has no power; it is the space of the eternal where we can sit without guilt, watch without purpose, listen with-out agenda, and play without a "why." Sabbath is the realm of the infant child whose world is only that of wonder, surprise, rest, nourishment and the delight of growing from the attention of love.

In our world of ever-increasing speed and constant change, is it possible to consider such an ancient and simple tradition as Sabbath as an element of living simultaneously? I suggest that it is not only possible, it is *essential*. Sabbath is a tradition that holds great hope for human progress and is the opportunity to practice the gift of freedom.

Freedom *from*

- the blaring demands of technology
- others who will not practice freedom
- noise that interrupts our island of stillness
- busy thoughts that invade our time of wonder
- guilt about taking time
- "static cling"

Freedom *for*

- a day for ourselves
- a day for others
- a day of wonder
- a day of play
- a day of activity
- a day of rest
- a day for family projects
- choosing one's tasks as one's pleasures
- something
- nothing

The Balance Practice—Play

If you ask a seven-year-old what he and his friends did all afternoon, the reply might very well be, "Nothing." That is because what seven-year-olds do together all afternoon, whether in the woods or in the garage, is such a natural part of their being that they do not distinguish it from who they are. Play and childhood are synonymous. Play is not something they "do"—it is a large part of who they *"are."*

Play is essential for the development of our complete selves. Researchers at Baylor College of Medicine found that children who do not play much develop brains 20 to 30 percent smaller than normal for their age. Rats that are raised with toys instead of in a sterile box environment have 25 percent more synapses per neuron. But play is even more than a critical and developmental component—it is a homecoming to our truest nature.

"There is an old Sanskrit word, *Lila,* which means play. Richer than our word, it means divine play, the play of creation, destruction and re-creation, the folding and unfolding of the cosmos. Lila, free and deep, is both delight and enjoyment of this moment and the play of God." (STEPHEN NACHMANOVITCH, *Free Play—The Power of Improvisation in Life and the Arts.*)

The playful mind acts from an inner necessity to create. When we create something new, it is not a creation of the intellect but a product from the natural instinct to play. We play and create to play. Fighting the gods of conformity, the great player improvises and loves the element of surprise. "Whether we are creating high art or a meal, we improvise when we move with the flow of time and with our own evolving consciousness, rather than with a pre-ordained script or recipe."(ibid)

Playing Alone

When was the last time someone knocked on our front door and asked us to come out and "play"? When I was growing up, my best friend, Billy Madison, lived across the street. Every day, Billy and I played together, but Billy was two years older than I, so the inevitable happened. One morning, as always, I went to Billy's door, knocked and asked his mother if Billy could come out and play. His Mom replied "no" to a very confused young playmate. "Bill started school today" she explained, "so you will have to play alone!"

It was as if the world of this three-year-old had come crashing down.

The words "School!" and "Play alone!" rang in my ears as I wandered back across the street. How could I play alone? What would I do? Little did I realize that I had just been taught one of life's great lessons by being challenged to discover the wonderful nature of solitude, individual creativity, and self-amusement. If we cannot play alone, we will never be a great playmate for anyone else.

One of the greatest fears in life is the fear of being alone, and this fear drives many people to re-marry or re-partner too soon after ending a relationship. Fear of being alone can encourage filling in the silent void with drugs, alcohol, or even a naturally induced depression. Does this fear relate back to being punished as a child and being sent to our room, alone? Are we so afraid of monsters and "things that go bump in the night" that we seek the comfort of another to protect us from these nightly visitors? Or are we afraid that if we ever get to know ourselves fully internally, we will discover that we are boring and someone with whom we would rather not spend time?

Regardless of the reasons for this fear, it is something we must confront and overcome in order to discover the reality that we are truly our own best friends and playmates. It is the ability to know each other's needs, wants, rhythms, fears, hopes, and dreams that makes any friendship last. Who knows that about ourselves better than we? We know what we want, when we want it, and how we prefer "its" delivery. Paying attention to "what we know" gives us an edge when we try to meet the needs of what we do not yet know. And again, who is better at self-discovery than that very self who searches those unknown areas?

As a highly extroverted "people-person," I actually enjoy interruptions. They break the tedium of even short-term routine and introduce an unplanned factor—usually the human factor. But I also need considerable time alone; that is my play time. Singing spontaneous songs at full volume as I drive my car, with my dog Bear sticking his head out the window, is a daily occurrence. I laugh at the absurdity of the exercise, and then do it again. I delight in early-morning coffee, a great cigar, naps after lunch, dancing wherever and whenever I hear a favorite song, talking in a variety of voices that say only "stupid things," arranging flowers for my home, rolling around on the floor with my dog, watching old videos and laughing with my children until we cannot breathe, and making faces in the mirror. These are all ways in which I play alone and have a wonderful time. If we take ourselves too seriously and disdain play as childish, we will not be able to return to that child within who does everything spontaneously and naturally.

Adults Find Play Difficult

Adults find play difficult. We not only allow barriers to play to emerge, we create them. Play is too threatening—it suggests vulnerability, openness, what we perceive as "foolish" behavior—and certainly it is not regarded as the best use of our time. Adults have lost the ability to *play without a "why!"* Instead, we must play for a reason: to socialize, to stay fit, to look good, to satisfy our needs to achieve and compete. When we can learn to roll down hills again, to skip down city streets if we feel like it, or organize "ring-o-leavio" games on hot summer nights in our neighborhoods, then we might have someone once again knock on our door and ask, "Can you come out and play?"

When parents play with their children, they create a lasting bond. Play is what the child wants and needs; play is also what the parent needs and may eventually want. When partners play, they create a magical bond that can be the key to being free, loving intimately, and living fully. It is an art form that can be lost in a relationship under pressure. Play has evidently been lost by the couple who sit in silence throughout their dining experience, able to engage only in a discussion of the menu. Play is absent as well from the couple who debates the smallest of details as if it held meaning of global proportion. Learning to play again, and accessing that childhood spot within the heart, can be a key to their renewal.

Ryan Ruch is a creative young man who at one time courted my daughter Laura. When Laura was feeling the pressure of exams at the end of her freshman year at university, her upper-classman boyfriend knew how to calm her tension. In the middle of her distress, he encouraged her to take an evening away from her study routine, and invited her to share a glass of wine "in front of a fire" in his fraternity house room. Using scrap wood, he constructed a fireplace in the corner. With black plastic bags serving as a firewall and the kindling neatly piled in a pyramid, a warm, red glow emerged from the center of the wood; this glow was a large, red drinking cup, lit up by a flashlight. Their creative evening became a much-needed elixir during a stressful time, and a perfect example of how to play.

Unfortunately, the adult world distinguishes play as separate from ordinary life. We compartmentalize within our work and relationships, having to make time for play. We create the rules: if you follow the rules, play continues; if you break the rules, the whistle blows, and play is stopped. And since we (as adults) have an inclination to break rules quite frequently, play is always in the process of being interrupted—*playus interruptus*. By contrast, animals and children flow with play, and play flows with them. My daughters were so successful at spending hours in their room "playing" that I remember standing quietly near their closed bedroom door, just to listen to what it was that they were actually creating. What I heard was earnest conversation about scenarios and characters that clearly were from *the dimension of pretend,* yet which were very real to them. There was no difference between this "play scenario" and their ordinary lives.

When we remember how to play, our bodies are re-membered. It is almost akin to getting new muscle tissue that once again allows the body to be agile and flexible. A seminar participant joined in a dance that the group was doing, but almost painfully. Dancing was not within his comfort zone, and it was very clear that it had been 45 years since his body had moved in that way. After a year's experience in movement and body therapy, and having let go of too many restrictive perceptions, this man now dances with fluidity and gusto; his body had to re-member what it felt like to be a child.

What would our relationships be like if we put play at the center of our lives? If play flowed in and out of us like a river, could it flush out the accumulation that clogs the creative and life-giving arteries? When couples first meet, their lives are filled with playful courting. They take the time for details, are willing to be spontaneous, and laugh as if it is the norm. When couples are in crisis, is it because they have allowed tedium to suggest that play is superfluous, or has tedium become dominant because they have not embraced play as the center of their lives?

Plato once said, "Life is to be lived as play!" What if our relationships knew play as a way to live a life fully expressed? Notes under the pillow, story-telling, long hugs in the kitchen, and plenty of laughter are all elixirs for the soul. The more we have of it, the more we crave it. Recently I watched an elderly couple walking down the street, holding hands. Just the sight of their affection was enough, but there was more. As they paused, peering into a large storefront window, she tickled him. He raised his arms, made the sound of a monster, and began to chase her. She hurriedly re-treated, making the appropriate squealing sounds. They played with aban-don, without caring one lick about what the world thought. I was so moved by this display of spontaneity that I skipped down the block.

Older than Culture

Play is older than culture. Creatures in the animal kingdom did not wait for humans to teach them how to express themselves playfully—they did it naturally. And when Homo sapiens finally arrived, no new features were added to the previously established format. For the animal or the child, play is instinctive—not something to be scheduled or compartmentalized for the purpose of balancing the frantic lives we know as adults.

Real play is based on the free-flowing and spontaneous eruption of cre-ative energy. It is the way of the playful Universe to flow, to create order out of chaos, and chaos from order. The only predictability of the Uni-verse is its unpredictable nature. Think of a collection of six-year-olds walking down the street: they divert from the path for a somersault in the yard, to smell a rose, skip, hop, or a tweak; yet they continue down the street in some fashion toward their destination. Likewise, the ever-expand-ing Universe continues on its own playful course—twisting, exploding, imploding, and creating anew every moment.

From Real Time to Beyond

Playful energy moves us out of "real time" into another dimension. I joined my associates Mary and Joy in North Carolina last summer to look at a piece of property that was a potential conference-center building site. The property's current inhabitant did not know the land was going to be up for sale, so we had to "sneak" onto this 900-acre farm, undetected. After skulk-ing around the property for a while—much more fun than the "usual way" of looking at property—we discovered a dilapidated log cabin by a rush-ing stream. With the cabin fueling our ever-increasing childlike imagina-tions, we pictured ourselves living in such a place a century ago.

In the stream were very large flat rocks that seemed to beckon us. Mary was the first to insist that we forge the stream and lie on the rocks. The practical, "real-time" side of me thought, "This could be a waste of time, we are going to get wet, we might get shot . . . and since both of them work for me, how much is this going to cost me per hour?" Busted! I was

54

trapped in my own adult-ness. So I shook off the tendency to be stuck and overly rational and forged the stream with enthusiasm. I made my way to "my rock" and lay back, watching the cloud formations pass by and listening to the sound of the rushing water swirl around our protected "islands." After lying there in silence for a half-hour, I knew that this was real play. We had returned to a dimension that we visited so often as children.

Laughter as Play

Laughter has a way of moving us to that "other" dimension instantly. Not only does the body become more healthy as a result of a great belly laugh, the mind also gets clear and the spirit becomes light. My friend Emily and I had just such an experience last year.

We were walking out of the meeting room for a lunch break during one of our Eagle Seminars. One of the participants casually said to me, "This is such an expanding experience." Feeling the extra poundage gained from the conference center's superb food, and without thinking, I quickly replied, "Kind of like what I'm doing in my pants." Both the participant and I chuckled. As we turned in the direction of yet another lunch array, I noticed a shocked look on Emily's face. "*What* did you say?" she questioned, her eyes wide. When I explained, she told me that she *thought* I had said, "I like what I'm doing in my pants!" To which I then retorted, "And I'm not finished yet!"

I am unsure whether it was the timing, the facial expressions or simply the levity of being in a favorite off-site setting, but we began to laugh so hard that muscles long-unknown to our skeletal systems seem to emerge. We gasped for air, trying to breathe in just enough to stay conscious while quizzical seminar participants passed us by, heading for lunch.

It did not end there. When we returned to my home the next day, another eruption of laughter occurred in the kitchen; I had to hold onto the counter to stay upright, even as my tear-swollen eyes caught a glimpse of Emily sliding down the wall toward the floor. At three o'clock the next morning, I heard gales of laughter emerging from the guest room down the hallway—Emily was continuing her pursuit of laughing herself to life. Of course, I joined the chorus from my room and eventually fell asleep again, perhaps an hour later. By the time Emily got on her flight back to Minneapolis later that morning, we were healthier than we had been in a long time. We had *played*.

Play At Work

If we really played at work, we could let go of the required holiday parties and mandatory celebrations, and see work as play. What is more fun than living our passion and doing what we love to do? When we do that, we are highly energetic, creative, and more able to laugh and enjoy life fully expressed. Even the tedium of long hours and deadlines becomes a part of "the game," if we can see our work as our play.

A successful interior designer in northern California told his staff to cancel all appointments they had for the next day, and to meet him at the office at 6:00 A.M.—in play clothes. They inquired about the reason but received no more information. Dutifully, they arrived the next morning to discover a stretch limousine waiting for them. Enjoying coffee and rolls along the way, they were driven north toward San Francisco on their mystery trip. The limousine pulled into the airport and they all boarded a flight to Los Angeles, where they were met by another limousine that deposited them at the gates to Disneyland. Asked what they were supposed to do there all day, their creative leader suggested the obvious: "Play!" So play, they did. Awakening their childlike spirit, this team of five had a marvelous experience that left them exhausted at the end of the day, yet they were still energized when they arrived back at the office by 10:00 P.M. that evening.

John Chambers, CEO of the very fast-paced and successful Cisco Systems, has integrated play and work in his own unique way. When people first meet John, they discover an energetic and superb leader, who truly loves what he does. Credited with the phrase *"Changing the Way We Work, Live, Play and Learn,"* John is the Internet visionary who is committed to expanding the possibilities for technology to enhance not only our work, relationships, and self-care, but the ways in which we play.

Recently I observed him in a large manager's meeting, speaking much like a preacher at a revival, captivating the crowd with his enthusiasm, his engaging presence, and his commitment to his message. He speaks with joy about his industry, which not only embraces change—it creates it. Challenging Cisco employees to work as teams and to "do more with less," he leads and inspires them by his own example. No one leaves the room untouched by the spirit of John Chambers.

I asked John how he balances his life in such a fast-paced world. "My family comes first," he said. "I give them my best. My son and I go fishing, and I spend as much time as I can at home. And I love what I do. My work is my passion, and I have a lot of fun doing my job." When I asked him how he cared for himself with so many demands on his time, his immediate response was, "Playing tennis. And I always play doubles, because I believe in the power of teamwork."

"What about the daunting challenge of the competition in your world of the Internet?" I asked, "doesn't that take away from the fun?" "I love the competition," he responded. "In fact, we want the competition to be good at what they do. It is more fun that way. Just like any competitive sport, if the other team is excellent, the game is more interesting. We have no desire to stomp out those who are in the field with us. We just want to win."

Play is truly at the heart of how one of the corporate world's most-admired leaders lives simultaneously—for he plays within his work, with his family, and in the care of his individual self.

Weaving the Seamless Fabric

Self-care just may be the most important element of *living simultaneously*. If we do not take the time to fill the well within, then what is left to bring to our relationships and to our work? We are a mini-Universe that reflects what swirls and changes around us, above us, before us, behind us and through us—each moment of every day. Living in harmony with the constant of change is not something to endure, it is an art form to embrace.

The Erotic Intelligence of our marvelous bodies has been given to us to awaken ourselves to the dream that is dreaming us. When we learn to taste the essence of life, feel the power of passion, smell the fragrance of love, hear the sound of a candle, and see the question of a child—then we are awakening to the wonderful story that lies ahead. Our lives are not filled with interruptions; they are a canvas of interruptions that shape the very picture that is our life.

Through the brilliance of the Mystical Mind, we learn to ponder the meaning of metaphor, discover the wisdom of story, and listen to the lessons that serve as our ongoing guides. Sacred Spirit collects all of this learning in the container of the soul and calls us to leave the weariness of depletion behind, to claim life in all of its fullness, change, and to breathe in the fresh air of renewal. Such a holy breath is for one purpose only: for living a life that is free for dedication to that which is sacred and a life that will soar on the wings of freedom.

Such is our life—to embrace—to live!

CIRCLE TWO

Relationships

Weaving the Seamless Fabric of Space for Love,
Love for Space, and Spacious Love

We cannot live only for ourselves. A thousand fibers connect us with our
fellow men; and among those fibers, as sympathetic threads, our actions run
as causes and they come back to us as effects. —HERMAN MELVILLE

The building and sustaining of relationships is the most difficult work we do. More involved than our self-care and more challenging than our jobs it is *the* lifelong opportunity for learning and personal growth. It is also the way we are reminded of our quantum existence. We do not stand apart from those with whom we share this planet. At some time or another, all of us are vendors, buyers, sellers, employees, and employers. Our consumption and our production depend on others. We are family, friend, neighbor, and child. We are a part of an interdependent network that we influence, just as we are influenced by it. Yet within this complex web of interdependence, the greatest challenge is to create a quality of space that allows further interdependence.

Limited space creates unhealthy dependence and vast expanses encourage unrealistic independence, but open space is the natural expanse created between atomic particles and is the way of the Universe. It is this kind of space that promotes the flexibility and lasting nature of human relationships.

Through the challenge of relationship, we can discover the following simple truths about what occurs when we limit space:

58

⚉ Attempting to change another person to fit our image is based upon our own judgment and fear.

⚉ When we avoid issues about ourselves that are discovered within an open-space relationship, we can be assured that these same issues will reappear in the reflective eyes of any future relationship.

⚉ If we seek relationships out of a need to be made whole by some external source, we create dysfunctional codependence.

It is only when relationships evolve from an open space of inner balance and fewer needs that they become a reflection of a holy union.

If we picture a quality relationship as an open space, there are grand views of the distant horizon that inspire the spirit. There is plenty of room to breathe and fresh air to encourage healthy growth. Although there are boundaries that require recognition and honor, nothing is cast in stone; we change each moment as we evolve. We do not own the space, for space cannot be owned; instead we create it and it creates us.

Let us examine three aspects within the circle of relationship that reflect the space metaphor:

⊠ Space for Love—Recreating Inner Space
⊠ Love for Space—Recreating Outer Space
⊠ Spacious Love—Creating Unlimited Space

⊠ SPACE FOR LOVE—RECREATING INNER SPACE

The challenge for any good parent is to provide an open space of trust, honor, and joy through which our children, as the most special guests in our lives, pass on their way to the rest of their lives. Any good relationship is dependent on the same kind of environment, for it must begin with an open and flexible space within us that ultimately creates the space around us. All of us have the potential to be like Charles Schulz's "Pigpen," projecting our dirt into the air around us, filling the outer space with internal litter. Instead, we can create a healthy outer environment by reflecting the quality of a renewed and healthy inner space.

This section will examine three components essential for recreating our inner space: Trust, Honor, and Reverence.

Trust

Living in the San Francisco Bay Area for the past 25 years, I have learned what "shaky ground" really means. Any structure built without more-than-adequate foundational support will eventually end up as rubble. We put great trust in the engineers and construction workers who erect our bridges and buildings.

When we discover that meaningful work is primarily based upon good relationships, we trust ourselves and encourage others rather than control them. When this occurs, organizations become more efficient and profitable by spending less money on hierarchical supervision and other subtle signs of mistrust. Trust is the solid foundation that upholds every aspect of relationship. When any relationship shares this foundation of trust, there is no need to wonder or worry about the intention of the other. Thus, in trusting, we take our first step in creating that internal open space.

My relationship with my children exemplifies how I create a trusting bond. As toddlers, my daughters would stand on the palm of my hand, balancing precariously while they learned to trust their father's strength and sustained support. I had to trust my ability to hold them without dropping them, just as they had to learn to trust me not to let them fall. As they grew into adolescence, they were challenged to "make good" by trusting their own judgment, instead of being told what to do. When they failed, they learned from their mistakes. They were trusted to live life fully, always knowing they could seek advice if they chose.

A neighbor's 15-year-old daughter stole and subsequently totaled her car. When my neighbor asked me how I had prevented such occurrences with my daughters, I reflected on her question and determined that it must have been because I taught the girls to drive on country roads when they were about ten years old. They never needed to steal a car for a "joy ride;" they could drive there, with me, any time they wanted.

A friend of mine has loved a woman for many years. He once regarded her as "the love of his life," but she may never be his lifelong partner because they lack trust. She does not trust him because of his temporary, yet untimely absence from her life while she faced some great losses. He does not trust her because, ultimately, she ended their relationship to begin another. Although there is still deep love and honor in their relationship, without trust, a future together is questionable.

Telling the Truth

Truth hurts, not the searching after, the running from. — JOHN EYBERG

The foundation of trust must allow room for the ubiquitous guest: truth. To tell the truth, the whole truth, and nothing but the truth—to ourselves, our partners, our children, a stranger or even the IRS—is almost a lost art form. Yet when we are able to tell what is true, we build relationships of trust, not only with others but with ourselves as well. When we can face self-truth without self-deception, we create the space to explore further what could, in fact, be true in other life arenas.

Truth-telling is not necessarily a popular practice. Bishop James Pike, a former Episcopal Bishop of the Diocese of California used to say that his mission was to "comfort the afflicted and to afflict the comfortable." When eventually tried for heresy because of his theological views that "afflicted the comfortable," he did not waiver from his position. Whereas centuries ago he may have been burned at the stake, in this case, he chose to wander into the desert, never to return.

Novelist Flannery O'Connor once wrote, "You shall know the truth and the truth shall make you odd." Truth-telling can make us stand so apart from the norm of deceit that we may be considered odd for being honest. When we invite others into the same odd, open space, we can hear without being defensive, and receive them without fear. We know that intimacy in relationships is not possible unless we can tell the truth; but telling the truth can greatly threaten that intimacy. The desire to be honest and the desire to be loving sometimes appear to be contradictory goals.

Truth spoken but not received is still truth; truth spoken *and* received is an expression of trust. When behavioral change for the good occurs, truth can become magic. Truth-telling sometimes needs to be forcefully dramatic. Interventions around alcoholism, violence and drug use are very dramatic ways to open the space for someone finally to hear what is true. Some of us require less drama to open our hearts to what we already "know we know" but resist acknowledging. We often hold ourselves together through avoidance and denial; here truth can often be painful and, in contrast, can break us wide open.

When I initiated my divorce proceedings 11 years ago, a close friend challenged me on my decision to end the marriage. I responded defensively, "But Beth, this is so common," to which she retorted, "That's just the point Jeff—I never expected *common* from you." I heard the truth then, and because of that one stinging experience, I am now more committed to excellence in relationship than ever before.

If truth really does "set us free," why is it that we avoid it? Why are we so afraid of being illuminated by the light of "what is"? Is the shadow of "what isn't" more attractive? Perhaps lying has become the norm, and self-deception a way of staying sane. Another possibility is our sense of loyalty. We remain loyal to an abusive source that has infiltrated our subconscious mind with powerful, often frequent and emotional messages. Even though the source has caused significant damage to our psychic health, somehow we remain loyal to this abuser or abusive belief. Denial is easier because truth-telling demands hard work. However, *living simultaneously* requires truth, and trust demands it.

An Example

Some years ago I was hired by a board of directors to "fix" the CEO of a small Silicon Valley company who, while successful at his job, was just plain mean. Working together seemed almost an impossibility, but for some reason he accepted the challenge. When I showed up on the appointed day to begin the coaching process, he looked at me and said, "What do you want?" I retorted, "I'm here to spend the day with you." "Lucky me," said the CEO. He then told me he had no time for me, but that if I had to spend the day, I could sit on the couch in his office while he did his "real" work.

An hour-and-a-half later, he seemed troubled by the fact that I sat watching him speak on the phone and interact with people who came into his office. Watching his behavior gave me insight into his inner self. Putting down the phone, he looked me in the eye, and again, assuming an intimidating tone asked, "What is it that you want?" "Just one thing," I responded; "If you answer one question, I will leave." "Good" he said. "It's a deal. Anything to get rid of you. What's the question?" "After watching and listening to you for the last ninety minutes," I said, "I want to know—what is the source of all your pain?" He looked at me as if his heart had been pierced. Silence gripped the room.

He sat for awhile, then put his feet on the desk which he had used as a protective barrier between us all along, and stared out the window. While he appeared to be considering the question, more minutes of silence passed, as the tension in the room increased. Since he had agreed to our "deal," he had to answer my question. I waited, entering his incubation process.

Finally, he broke the silence. Turning to me, he said, "I've only told this story once before, and that was to my wife." I waited with expectation. "When I was 16 years old, my 'old man,' in one of his drunken stupors, threw me out of the house. He said, 'You're nothing but a bum, your mother and I never wanted you, and you'll never amount to anything. Get out!' So I did," he said. "I left that day and never saw my old man again. I would see my mother on occasion, but as far as I was concerned, I had no father."

Silence again filled the room as we each felt the gut-wrenching pain of that deep wound. I felt great appreciation for this old warrior, who was finally able to remove the lid he had kept on his pain for so many years. Now exposed, his pain was evidence that *he had become loyal to an image created by his father.*

Those hurtful words and that experience of rejection became the substance of his life's purpose. From the age of 16, he was determined to prove to his "old man" that he was "Somebody." He would become successful, but out of spite and hatred. After years of using his amassed power to frighten others and confronting everyone as an adversary, he had perfected his father's abusive style. He had mastered the art of hiding the fear that he was "not enough" by projecting an image of toughness and meanness. And he became just like the one he had abhorred.

Seeing that he had wasted too much of his 61 years combating his now-dead father and that his life still had great possibilities, I decided to challenge the loyalty and the image that had ruined his life. I stood up from his couch. He stood up from behind his desk, probably assuming that his intrusive visitor was leaving. I said, "Come here." He said, "Why?" "Just come here," I responded. Surprisingly, almost dutifully and with head down, he started to walk toward his challenger. When he got to within two feet of me he stopped. Putting my hands his shoulders, I looked into his eyes and said: "Son, I am so sorry for what I have done. Your mother and I are so proud of you. We love you very much."

The stunned expression on the face of this beleaguered CEO, whose eyes resembled those of a deer frozen in a vehicle's headlights, seemed to say, "I can't believe that you just said that." Then he began to cry. At first, tears simply rolled down his cheeks, but then quiet sobs began to emerge from deep within. Purging the pain of 45 years, his body began to convulse with sobbing so deep that he collapsed into my arms. I had to hold up this old, "toughened warrior" as a few people passed by the windows of his office and witnessed this dramatic event.

Six months later he retired from his company. He handed over the power and responsibility to three vice-presidents who until then had been puppets on his string, and he began to travel with his wife. To this day I will occasionally receive a post card from somewhere in the world with six words on it: "Thank you, Thank you, Thank you." It is our code, and a way of knowing that all continues to be well.

Embracing the Messenger

When we can hear truth and appreciate the courage of the messenger, the practice becomes easier for both the sender and the receiver. The expressed truth becomes a nonjudgmental message that simply gives feedback regarding a perception that differs from our own. And when expressed with love, it creates change. A friend who is a priest used to enjoy shocking her congregation by stating, "God does not forgive!" As expected, the congregation would sit in silence, choking on the comment. Just for effect, she would repeat it. When she felt that the tension was high enough, she would explain that if we truly believe in a relationship built upon unconditional love and trust, there is no need for forgiveness—because there is no judgment.

Mark, my office manager, appeared unannounced at my home one evening at dinner time. He sat down on the patio and said, "I've come to tell you about a mistake I have made." Sitting face to face with me, he admitted his failure and acknowledged his responsibility in resolving it. Although I might never have known about the mistake otherwise, Mark told the truth. Our relationship enjoys trust, and this incident contributed to an even deeper foundation.

My relationship with another associate, Emily, is a friendship built upon 20 years of trusting each other to tell the truth. With great care, Emily will challenge me to look at situations from another perspective. Usually with less care and more bravado, I will challenge Emily to claim the magnitude of her gifts and to dance with abandon.

Is there anything that our children could do that would ever cause a permanent separation from us? Loving one's children unconditionally and letting them pursue their own paths, without controlling them is a parent's challenge. Their life paths are their own, and differ from those of their parents.

This does not mean that we let a six-year-old walk in front of a train. We guide children in their early years, teaching them to navigate so that we can let them go. Criticism will only stop them in their tracks, and advising them without their invitation will only impose our own agendas on them. Loving them means there is no need for forgiveness because we do not judge them according to standards of "who we think they should be." This builds the foundation of trust for a rich, lifelong relationship.

Honor

A billionaire businessman from Singapore once commented, "What is most important to me is being honorable in everything that I do." His simplistic and powerful testimony has had a profound effect on how the Patnaude companies do business.

What would our lives be like if everything we did was honorable? The application of this life rule to every situation, every act, every communication, every intention—even every thought—is something we have come to expect only of saints. Yet none of us want an epitaph that says, "She was efficient!" Instead we prefer, "She was a woman of honor."

When we honor the special guests in our lives with whom we develop relationships, we give them one of life's greatest gifts—the room to be authentically who they are. Such a relationship develops an attitude of reverence and a willingness to honor each other's boundaries.

The poet Rainier Rilke described intimacy as being "the guardians of each other's boundaries." In a relationship that enjoys such honor, we join our partner at the edge of our individuality, in mutual protection of each other's boundaries. Thus, we are not alone in this important work.

The Kidney-Bean Model

Let's look at what could be called the "kidney-bean model" of relationship. Instead of viewing intimacy as two circles becoming one ("the clump"), or even two entities creating shared space ("the suffocation model"), Rilke's statement could best be described as two kidney beans, side by side—two individuals, uniquely created and living on purpose, coming together. Connected at the top and bottom, they are one, yet distinctly two. Their boundaries are clearly defined and their positions allow each to observe and protect the other. In the center is open space, where there is freedom for anything to happen—initiated by one, the other, or both. It is a meeting place of mind, body and spirit.

The Inner Boundaries

Time and Space ⚸ Personal space and time honor individual need. We all need our own individual time for refreshing and refilling, in addition to more conventional vacations together. Couples can make time for separate holidays or renewal times. Women and men each need their own sacred space to which they can retreat, display their personal sacred objects and be alone. Each partner can work toward helping ensure this for the other.

At work, individual time is required for each of us to perform our tasks and fulfill our purpose. Too much time spent in meetings is tiring and invades the time each of us needs for doing what still remains to be accomplished individually. Cubicles are industry's way of providing some personal space while at the same time remaining efficient. When a way is found to avoid the intrusiveness of sound and easy access, the work area will honor the needs of the individual more effectively.

Fantasies and Daydreams ⚸ We all need to express ourselves, whether through daydreams or action. Criticism shuts down our expressive process, so we may go elsewhere, where our musings will be received. To be encouraged to dream our dreams, without being labeled as "flighty" or "a dreamer," feeds the soul as well as expands the mind and is a characteristic of a great teacher.

Kingsford Jones (known to friends as "King"), a young attorney and father of two boys was an example of such a teacher. One day when he was in the middle of a group meeting at his home, his son Wyatt came in and complained that his older brother Leslie had ridiculed him about his theory. "What theory is that?" asked King. "Since earthworms move through the dirt, you should be able to hear them if you really listen," said Wyatt. "What a fascinating idea," said Kingsford to his hopeful son. "Let's go see." King turned to those gathered and asked for permission to leave for a few minutes in order to attend to the business at hand. Instead of continuing our business, the group watched the far-more-interesting investigation.

King and Wyatt proceeded to the front yard and each put an ear to the ground expectantly. Moving from place to place, they listened carefully for the sound of an earthworm moving slowly through the dirt below. All of a sudden they ran into the house, only to emerge equipped with drinking glasses that they then used as earphones. The image of this father-and-son team moving about the yard with drinking glasses held to their ears and pressed to the ground was even more rich now. After a few more minutes of excited investigation, they returned to the house and announced to their fascinated onlookers that they had, indeed, heard earthworms. We all left that meeting inspired about ways we could encourage the questions of children and be future participants in their discoveries.

Needs and Wants ⊠ All of us have needs; all of us have wants. Determining the difference is an individual's challenge, but honoring each is the responsibility of the guardian. Most us want relationships, but not everyone needs them on the same level; some of us are content with solitude and the satisfaction of our own company. All of us have needs related to food, clothing, shelter, and bodily functions, yet the desire for more than what is "necessary" is one of the major reasons for lives being out of balance. Excessiveness or "moreitis" can claim our souls and affects the health of our planet as consumerism reigns. *Living simultaneously* means making choices between what is needed and what is wanted.

The motives for achievement, affiliation, and power, as described in an up-coming section, are based upon need. Understanding what level of need exists in ourselves and others helps us create the open space for others to behave without our judgment. My two daughters, both now in their 20s, were raised under the same roof but they each have differing needs. Laura sets high standards for achievement and is very hard on herself when she does not meet them; meanwhile, happy with occasional success, Julie does not feel the need for high achievement. Laura has people all around her, while Julie is more content with her "aloneness." Although each has a strong need for power and making a difference, Julie's arena is more concerned with global issues, while Laura is more localized in her outlook. Understanding their varying needs has helped me be a better parent to each of them.

Reverence

One of my associates, Margaret More, is an extraordinary teacher; beyond that, she is a grandmother like no other. During a summer vacation two years ago at Lake Tahoe, she informed her five-year-old grandson Wilson that, on the eve of the full moon, they would celebrate an "ancient ritual" enjoyed by every grandmother and grandson since time began: They would rise just before midnight, go down to the edge of the lake and sing a *wishing song* to the moon. As they waited expectantly for the full moon to hover over this pristine mountain lake, their excitement grew. Finally, the evening arrived. Just before midnight, Margaret gently nudged Wilson out of a deep sleep and informed him, "The full moon is waiting." The little boy quickly shook off sleep, leapt to his feet, and the two began their journey down the path to the lake, guided by the light of the full moon in the clear mountain air. As they reached the water's edge and the brilliant moonlight streamed across the lake to illuminate the participants in this "ancient ritual," Wilson turned to his grandmother and said, "Granny, I know you do this kind of thing all of the time, but I have a feeling that tonight is going to change the rest of my life. What wishing song should we sing?" "You choose," said Margaret. And choose he did. Holding hands, standing in the full light of the summer moon's radiance, they began: "We wish you a Merry Christmas. . . ."

As Rabbi Abraham Heschel said, "Awe is the beginning of wisdom." When we experience the sensation of breathless awe, whether in front of a daVinci painting or a full moon crafted by Divine intelligence, we experience the sacred. When we open the door to a realm beyond knowledge, we experience wisdom. But if awe is the beginning of wisdom, and wisdom the completion of awe, then *reverence must be the beginning of awe.*

For 25 years, I have held the curious title of "The Reverend." Others in this profession are known as "The Very Reverend," "The Right Reverend," "The Most Reverend" or even "The Most Right Reverend." Yet title alone does not determine posture or practice. Reverence is an attitude, a way of being, a willingness to seek the Divine in all things. The Hindu practice of bowing to another and offering the word "Namaste" means, "I reverence the light within you." This is a simple reminder that we are all light bearers and worthy of another's recognition

Imagine a relationship between loving partners, each holding a reverence for the other. This does not mean deference—a walking behind—but equality: side-by-side, shoulder-to-shoulder. This relationship is characterized by an appreciation for each other's thoughts; a willingness to allow each other the room to dream; a willingness to listen as if everything matters; and a commitment to guard the boundaries that protect each other's precious self.

In the *Old English Book of Common Prayer*, the exchanged marriage vows included, "I reverence thy body." In a world where sexual assault and date rape has become all too common, the concept of revering another's body as a sacred temple may seem foreign. But it is that for which we each long.

What if . . . everyone, whether at work or at home, was viewed as a holy and sacred creation? What if . . . we truly viewed our individual selves as the same? What if . . . our neighborhood communities were seen as tribes to which we belonged and in which we shared not only meals, but lawn tools? What if . . . our cities and towns were examples of honest and good government, where trust, honor and reverence were the norm? What if . . . our nations all stopped posturing against one another and reverenced the integrity of different traditions? What if . . . we saw our *planeta* (from the Latin, meaning 'wanderer') as a holy vehicle hurtling through space as if it had a purpose and destiny of its own to fulfill?

Seeing differently can mean acting differently. *Acting with reverence is the beginning of awe—awe is the beginning of wisdom.*

⊠ LOVE FOR SPACE—RECREATING OUTER SPACE

We shape our dwellings and afterward, our dwellings shape us.
—WINSTON CHURCHILL

Perhaps one of the reasons people spend so much time at work is because, at least there, they have a physical space of their own. It may simply be a cubicle surrounded by ever-present noise and interruptions, yet at the very least, it is one's own space. Adorned perhaps with only pictures, computer, phone, and files, the workspace is not a *unique* space, yet it does become a *private* space. For the sake of relationship, the moment many people leave work and enter the door to their home, they sacrifice their private space for that shared space.

Traditionally, men have carved out some form of private space for themselves. With women often finding their only refuge in the kitchen or sewing room, men have had the garage, workshop, basement, den, or home office to dream their dreams and enjoy their solitude. This inequality is no longer acceptable; personal space is so necessary that every individual must learn to claim and create his or her own sacred space.

69

Many relationships could be enhanced if partners lived apart or had their own separate dwellings. What if our homes were built with smaller but separate sleeping quarters for each adult? Each person within the relationship could enjoy his or her private space, yet they could be together whenever they chose. I may sound too much like a bachelor (with a home just the way I want it), but I believe that if it were affordable, having separate homes might be even better. If I ever partner again, it may be with that idea in mind.

Think how natural our appreciation for space was as children. When my siblings and I were children, we would make "leaf houses" by raking all the autumn leaves into separate "rooms" and then play "house." Snow forts, blanket forts, or the once-in-a-lifetime refrigerator box home were all spaces we designed for play and creativity.

In one of our seminars, my associates and I ask participants to describe one of their "childhood spots." Often befuddled by the challenge, many have to search back to what actually was a space for dreaming dreams and making plans, and a place where they could be alone. I built a tree house, where I would concoct all kinds of schemes. Unfortunately, I built it in a tree on five acres of vacant property that belonged to someone else who eventually made me remove it. Tearing down my creative space was a painful operation but only affirmed the importance of personal space at an early age.

Growing up in a household of two parents and six children, it was necessary to have a place of my own, where I could enjoy being alone with myself and my dreams. I played alone for hours in the basement of our home, where there was a large bench for my father's tools and my older brother's chemistry set. It was my childhood respite, an arena for creativity, and a place for the practice of play.

Just as an outstanding teacher pays attention to every bit of detail in order to create the ultimate learning environment, we each need to pay attention to the spaces where we work and live. Colors, natural light, texture, lighting, furniture and its placement all contribute toward creating a space that will shape our attitudes and our well-being.

Perhaps unknowingly, we each have a love for our own private spaces because they are also spaces that we can recreate in our own image. Unlike the basement that I needed to leave intact—to give the impression that I had not meddled in my father's or brother's treasures—my bedroom was a sacred spot that I could recreate in any way I chose. It contained a large, old chair in which I would sit by the window and read selections from the bookcase nearby. There was a desk at which I would write term papers at the final hour. A back stairway to the kitchen below served as a late-night entrance if I came home past curfew. It was also a place where friends of like-mind gathered.

Howie Hopkins, Billy Madison, and Tommy Pratt were frequent visitors who had the privilege of entrance because they were members of a band that would practice for hours behind the closed doors of my bedroom. With drums, amplifiers, and guitars positioned wherever they could fit, it was in this room where we made music and where music made us. This art form became such a part of our lives that we eventually had several bands and wrote numerous songs. One of our members, Gary Raynor, even made it to the "Big Time," playing for years with Sammy Davis, Jr. That bedroom somehow had an influence upon all of us, shaping the emerging personalities who have all gone on to "make a difference."

Symbols

Have nothing in your house you do not know to be useful or believe to be beautiful. —HENRY DAVID THOREAU

By placing in an outer, open space those symbols that represent some part of who we are, we make that space uniquely our own. When I enter someone's office, cubicle or home, I always notice what symbols are present that speak of his or her interior life. The collection is as unique as the individual. One corporate client whom I coached moved from Austin, Texas, to Sunnyvale, California, to take a new position as a vice president. Six months after her appointment, she still had no symbols in her local office that indicated that she had arrived. Her walls were blank and her desk and shelves had nothing representing her. Her staff indicated to me that they felt "she wasn't available." I suggested to her that she spend a weekend at her home, unpack boxes and bring some symbols to her office to let her staff know that she was present and there to stay.

I spend a great deal of time in my office, which is a converted garage. When it was still a dark, cold, and very cluttered habitat for spiders and mice, I brought a friend in to see this "future office" at my newly purchased home. In a characteristic "cup is half-empty" manner she exclaimed, "You have to be crazy if you think you can convert this dump!" Undaunted by such negativity, I went on to create a most beautiful space, filled with symbols that represent who I am.

The white walls, carpet, and cabinets are a statement about order and cleanliness. Two skylights allow natural light in while three different lighting systems create multiple lighting effects. The Oriental carpet reminds me of the importance of history and excellence in the quality of work. An L-shaped glass desk surrounds me, yet its transparency encourages me to be seen as I am. Paintings full of color and life hang on the walls while countless photographs of my three best friends—my children and our dog— are at eye-level beyond the oversized computer screen. Framed works of wisdom are placed strategically, as if to keep me on track when the sound of my two antique clocks ticking away draws me back to my father's jewelry store, where I worked as a child. A small fountain trickles in the background, next to a large rose from my garden, displayed in a crystal stem vase. The couch and chair offer comfort to any guest. Our golden retriever, Bear, sleeps by my feet, breathing almost in sync with the classical music emanating from the CD player. The shelves of books—each one earmarked like an old friend or teacher—are probably the most indicative of how I think and what I believe. My home, likewise, has countless reflections of my beliefs and values.

Look at what surrounds you and the details you have chosen to acknowledge your values and your beliefs. Does the outer space that you have shaped suggest order, excellence, lasting quality and a colorful life reflective of an inner balance, or does it show that you choke on disorder and clutter?

Clutter

If we fill our outer space with so much "stuff" that a quality of openness is diminished, then there is no room for spirit to flow and create. I have a life-guideline that keeps things simple: "If I don't know I have it, I don't need it." This stems from an inner desire for simplicity and order, thus reflecting an outer behavior. I periodically go through my files and if I discover something I had forgotten, I obviously don't need it, so out it goes for recycling. Occasionally, I will discover something I have needed but couldn't find, but that is different. Most of us accumulate much more than we need, and so clutter starts to have its insidious effect upon us.

Kitchen counters seem to have a magnetic quality that shouts out, "Put it here!" I had one corner that used to build clutter as if it were propagating overnight. No matter what I used to do to avoid it, clutter was winning the battle. I finally designated one top drawer as my "clutter drawer," into which I daily sweep everything that has escaped the trash or recycling. Although I have imagined hearing quiet laments of resignation coming from that drawer during the night, I have held my resolve and kept clutter where it belongs.

One of the biggest channels for clutter is the U.S. Postal Service. Dedicated to deliver not only through rain, sleet, and snow, they also are obliged to deliver anything and everything that bears a stamp in their name—and the onslaught seems to get worse if you make any request to be taken off a junk-mailing list! The issue is easily resolved by walking from the mailbox to the garbage or recycling bin. What is important is opened, and the only items that make it to my desk is something that requires a response.

One of the places often hidden from the public eye is the bedroom. There is a good reason for this—it's full of clutter. This is one of the worst places to keep out of order, since it affects our sleeping patterns. If we sleep in a room of chaotic accumulation, we surround ourselves with an energy that will disrupt even the soundest sleeper.

A very close friend lives her life in a flurry of chaos. She never knows where anything is, is almost always late for every meeting, misses making house and car payments regularly and has every newspaper and magazine from the past six months stacked in her kitchen. She has to react to the surprises of every day because she has not been able to cross over to being proactive. In asking me what she could do to achieve some semblance of balance in her life, the first step was a discussion about what she valued that made her seek such a change. The second step was quite obvious and was an outer action—de-clutter and reorganize her space so that it brought her some peace, rather than chaos. It made a difference, and today she attributes her increased sense of inner balance to not letting the accumulation of external clutter build up.

The Spiritual Village

Being such an avid proponent of *creating space that eventually creates us*, I am now beginning to develop a dream that I have had for a long time—building a spiritual conference center in a pattern of circles. Unlike the villages

73

of the past that were built around squares—a town square, and a street grid design with a square cathedral or municipal building in the center—the Spiritual Village breaks "out of the box" by having an ancient labyrinth at its center. To be used as a training center for various seminars on enhancing life and spirit, the labyrinth center will be a large building with a sacred geometry that "works" each participant just by his or her being inside. Around the entrance of the round center building is a circular garden that actually recreates the path of a simple labyrinth. Participants therefore must walk the maze before and after each session, since this pathway is the only way in and out of the center. Care must be given to time and thoughts as people make their way to and from the seminars.

Around the garden is the third circle—a village round—a cobblestone street that will serve as an arena for art shows, markets, and outdoor cafes where people gather for dialogue and community celebrations. The fourth circle is composed of the actual French-cottage homes where participants in the seminars are housed, thus creating, in part, the ever-changing village community. The fifth circle encompasses the entire open space of 40 acres of farmland that provides food as well as opportunities for seminar participants to work the land. Unlike anything ever created before, this center will serve as a reminder that we can move away from box-like compartmentalization toward the universal flow of the perfect circle. We can *shape our dwellings and eventually, our dwellings will shape us."*

⊠ SPACIOUS LOVE

In a word, there are three things that last forever: faith, hope and love; but the greatest of them all is love. —I CORINTHIANS 13:13

Love is the most potent source of power. It is available to all of us, all of the time, anywhere. To live *in love* is why we have been created—to receive love and to give love. Love invites response. The infant knows the adoring eyes of the parent and the tenderness of the parental voice; her presence, in return, gives the parent the first inkling of what real love means. The child that becomes more confident and powerful as the result of a household of love gives back to the home a playful spirit where laughter is the norm and souls are nourished. The employee who becomes more able to fulfill his or her passion and life purpose when working in an environment of love returns the gift through dedication and excellence. We are created to love and receive love—love responding to love is the center of creation—and when that occurs, life is expressed at its deepest level.

We know what it feels like when relational love is hauntingly absent. The pain of loneliness, abandonment, and emptiness lives deep within our gut and aches like no other pain. We long for the touch of skin against skin, lips upon lips, and bodies that spoon as if they were crafted for stacking. We also know the profound pain of love's absence from our work and from ourselves. We exist rather than live—we merely get through another day rather than celebrate life. Meaninglessness takes love's place and despair becomes a stultifying shadow.

We are the only creatures capable of self-deception. In love's absence, we seek money, sex, power, and security as a way to anesthetize ourselves, when all we really want is love. We conspire with delusion, believing that external things will fill the void, yet we know that is not true. We build colleges for studying war, yet have no universities dedicated to learning the more potent power source, love.

In the quantum world, love is a paradox. In any problem, love is the mysterious solution, yet we do not know how to get there. In every question, the answer lies hidden. In every pain, there is joy. In every celebration, there is heartache. When we seek love, love eludes us. When we are content to let love seek us, it finds us. Paradox reigns supreme.

Love is not romance—it is much more. The world seeks a cheap connection with the source by reducing it to steamy novels, daytime "soaps," magazine wisdom or Oval Office affairs. We consult our horoscopes for the perfect match, we await our soul mate's arrival from Mars or Venus. Yet romance only leads to disillusionment, as expectation leads to disappointment. Real love can be found lying at your feet.

Bear Dog Love

At my feet is the fullest expression of unconditional love that I know—my Golden Retriever, Bear, who certainly looks like a dog but actually is my spiritual director. If I can someday grow up to be like this six-year-old wonder, then I will have discovered the true meaning of love. Consider this:

If we could

- start the day without caffeine or pep pills,
- not rely upon alcohol to relax or sedatives to sleep,

- ❀ always be cheerful and not complain,
- ❀ understand when our loved ones are too busy to give us their attention,
- ❀ overlook another's frustration when taken out on us,
- ❀ ignore one's educational or economic status,
- ❀ live without self-deception, lying, or prejudice,
- ❀ take criticism without blame or resentment,
- ❀ gratefully eat the same food every day for all of our lives, then we are almost as good as our dogs. (ANONYMOUS)

The spacious love that I experience from Bear includes three consistent factors: attraction, attention and acceptance. His attraction for me occurs at the gate when he expectantly awaits the first scratch at the end of the day. He leans against my leg while I talk to a neighbor or plops his head on my lap as I watch the news. He will interrupt chewing or napping to walk to the office door window to peer in for just a glance, then returns to his work. The attraction, from both sides, is obvious.

When Bear is not sleeping, his purpose appears to be watching my every move. Moving about the house, he places himself wherever he can watch, usually right in the pathway of any activity. He has the innate ability to place his body exactly where my foot needs to be. I have not experienced such direct eye contact from most humans as when he looks deep into my eyes, as if he is searching for a glimpse of my soul. One call or whistle and he bounds forth, attentive and willing for whatever may ensue. Such attention seems inordinate in the life of a human, but not in the realm of a dog.

The ultimate gift given to me by this 100-pound blonde is that of acceptance; there is no pretense in this relationship. Bear knows every mood, every quirky nuance of my behavior—and it makes no difference. Though I change, he remains consistently the same. He loves me as I am and sometimes, in spite of who I am. He has no concept of forgiveness, since he makes no judgments. With him I can sing with abandon, dance as if no one is watching, and celebrate with foolishness. Oh, to be so free in full view of humans!

Spacious love is not only about deepening our relationship with another person—a soul mate, a partner. Our society may focus perhaps too much on "coupling," which becomes too narrow a pathway for a power that truly knows no limits. Spacious love is also about our relationships with our work mates, our neighborhoods, our cities, our homeless, our land—even loving the unlovable parts of ourselves. It is about expressions of intimacy that are not romantic or dyadic. When we become more loving of all that surrounds us, love will beat a path to our door and the world will change.

Spacious Love will consider three aspects of this potent power that is a part of every type of relationship of love: *Attraction, Attention and Acceptance.*

Attraction

We each see things differently. Reality has been described as seeing things not as they are, but as we are; thus we see what we are looking for. If a horticulturist and a developer are looking at the same plot of land, they will each have a different perception of the land's use. People who have a "victim" mentality see problems as a universal plot against them, while the optimist sees a problem as an opportunity. The mystery of attraction is equally as individual.

The Greeks defined *eros* as the power that draws us to an object we believe will complete us. Plato created the Myth of Androgyny to illuminate this fact. Once, human beings were joined back-to-back in three combinations: male-to-female, male-to-male, and female-to-female. The pairs could move about by turning cartwheels on their four arms and legs but were frustrated because they could not turn and face each other. Zeus intervened by splitting the pairs with a thunderbolt. Since that time, each of the pair has sought its other half; thus, the combinations of men and women, men and men, women and women. According to the Platonian myth, our pain of separation was healed by the god Eros.

There is often a hunger and an urgency in erotic attraction, and we are not content until we get what we want. The Buddha said, "Desires are inexhaustible." The power of desire is not psychological, it is ontological—deeply rooted in the essence of who we are. Once we "get what we want," we move on to our next quest. Desire is the essential human experience, our passion, our life-energy. It is foolish to try and suppress what is our nature. What is needed is the wisdom to know what is good for us and what is not.

Fifteen years ago, I was told of a car that was for sale—a red-with-white-inserts, 1957 Corvette that was in cherry condition. I knew it was not feasible to consider such a purchase but *just looking at it* would do no harm. Walking toward the garage where it had been housed for several years, I could feel my heart pounding and my pulse rate quickening. It was as if a past love had returned to my life and awaited our reunion. As the door slowly opened and I caught the first glimpse of that radiant red creation, I was finished. Nothing could keep me from owning that vehicle— lust filled every cell of my body, my head swooned and my heart leapt. It proved to be the right response since the car brought joy to many who saw it, used it, and remember it to this day. Eventually sold some years later for three times what it cost, it became the down payment on a summer home that my children will leave to their children. Lust can be good.

Two years ago, I was about to leave a rather uninspiring party when a younger woman, whom I had seen earlier but had dismissed as someone's date, walked up and began talking to someone in front of me. The moment she spoke, I became engaged. I could feel the pheromones catapulting out of every pore—I visually inspected every part of her physical self, the sound of her voice was full of enthusiastic spirit—I was sure that I could smell her sweet fragrance strategically applied and it was only the sensations of taste and touch that longed for expression. I was smitten.

Why are we attracted to that which we seek? Proximity, physical attractiveness, and similarity are the most common factors. Arousal can also occur by excitement and crisis. Being with someone during a natural disaster or a life-threatening event often creates deep and lasting bonds. But we also are attracted to those relationships that we know won't work. We chase after them because there is no chance of their succeeding and if there is sudden reciprocity, we turn and run. Is this attraction truly to make ourselves whole, as Plato suggests? Is that not a co-dependence, which we have been clearly warned about by modern psychology as a pathway toward dis-ease? Or is having clarity about our desires and needs a refreshing stance in a world of pretense and societal expectation?

The authors of *Sleeping with Bread: Holding What Gives You Life* write: "The pattern of feeling ashamed of my needs and desires is an aspect of co-dependency. I behave like a co-dependent whenever I orient myself around the reality of others rather than living in my own reality and honoring my needs. Many people working in the field of addictions are saying that co-dependency and the core emotion of shame underlie all other addictions." Desire is a part of the human condition and clarifying those de-sires is a step toward wholeness and inner balance.

What are the dynamics that make attraction such a unique preference? Certainly the five senses comprise the first level of screening. I may sound typically male here, because for me, visual attractiveness can be a first level of engagement. When the attraction is to other human being, merely one dissonant factor can bring the attraction to a screeching halt. My personal assessment includes one's tone of voice. In the past, when invited to meet that perfect someone, I have had a phone conversation to determine not only attitude, but voice quality. If the voice tone doesn't suggest depth, mystery, enthusiasm, and sensuality, I conclude with an uncomfortable yet honest suggestion that I don't think we have enough in common and a po-lite, "good luck." My demanding proclivities have not always made the per-son on the other end of the line terribly happy.

I am not suggesting that we seek the fulfillment of all our desires at any cost. Desire is a two-headed coin—it can be either a blessing or a curse. It is a blessing if eros becomes a driving force toward the completion of our whole selves. Our attraction to erotic justice or compassion stems from a more universal understanding of eros without the sexual connotation that, unfortunately, has become the norm. Eros becomes the fire that fuels our life-purpose and moves us out of lethargy. The dark side of eros is addic-tion instead of pleasure, suffocation instead of satisfaction, destruction in-stead of wholeness.

THE PRACTICE OF RIGHT-DESIRE

What is right is often forgotten by what is convenient.
—BODIE THOEN

The Desire for Affiliation

As quantum people, we are interdependent beings. Eros is the power that drives us to seek the companionship of lovers, friends, and strangers—members of a community of which we are each a part. We are attracted to people, not out of lust or sexual gratification, but because of a deep desire to relate. Very few us of are hermits—instead, we seek connection and meaning in relationships.

Friendship is the highest quality of relationship. Lovers who are not friends rarely last as lovers. Families who do not share a friendship can become a collection of dispirited housemates. Work teams that do not develop friendships leave a powerful resource for creativity and productivity untapped. Jesus bestowed the highest praise upon his disciples when he said, "No longer do I call you my disciples, I call you my friends." I so honor the understanding of friendship that I have actually refused invitations to friendship. Such a relationship takes time, quality, and a commitment to be present. If I cannot do it well, then I choose not to begin.

Joyce is my friend. If a comparison of psychological type, background, education and career path were examined, she and I could not be more opposite. Yet what we have in common is a desire to be present for each other throughout the years, to communicate on a regular basis and to learn from each other. Although she has lived in Thailand for the last ten years, we maintain our friendship, unaffected by time and space. It is this practice of right-desire that calls us into relationships with others to satisfy our need and desire to relate.

The Desire for Achievement

The erotic desire to achieve is a practice of right desire. As we are attracted to successful people, we are also attracted to the force that calls us forward to become the fullest expression of our gifts and talents. Setting goals for ourselves and achieving them is one of life's greatest pleasures. With accomplishment comes satisfaction, and with satisfaction comes completion. And then we begin again.

Barbie Lussier is one of only 50 women in the United States who serves as a general contractor in the home-building industry. Her achievement began when she and her husband built a home near Sacramento ten years ago. After observing the process of the professionals building their home, she realized that organizing, managing schedules, and motivating people was what she did every day as a mother and spouse. She decided to follow her passion. Inspired to disprove the warnings from others that a woman could not achieve such a dream in a male-dominated industry, Barbie set out to become a successful builder. As only the Universe would have it, this builder-to-be soon thereafter found herself across the street from the American Builder's Convention in Los Angeles, while she and her family were visiting Disneyland. Instead of one day in the *Land of Make-Believe*, she sneaked into a *World She Believed She Would Make* and walked about the convention floor getting ideas. Last year (ten years later), she addressed The National Builder's Convention delegation as a Keynote speaker and as a recognized example of a successful woman builder.

This erotic passion for achieving a dream is the fire that creates legacies. Eros put us on the Moon, dug the Panama Canal, and built the Seven Wonders of the World. It is eros that will guide each one of us toward what we define as success. Right-desire is not achievement-at-any-cost and the destruction of anyone or (anything) that gets in achievement's way—it is the building of dreams through the use of our talents that makes the world a better place.

The Desire for Power

Power is one of the most misunderstood aspects of eros. Misuse of power, as in the misuse of achievement or affiliation, is a corruption. Power, in and of itself, is not. It is the vehicle for positive influence that brings about necessary change.

The Corporate world seeks to empower work teams for high performance and autonomy. Sports teams seek not only superior talent, but those who will lead and influence others as well. Without the right-desire for power, Martin Luther King, Jr. would have been a very senior Baptist minister, Mother Theresa would have been a devout hermit, and Rosa Parks would have ridden in the back of the bus. Erotic power calls us to the front of the bus, and with unquestionable authority declares, "No, I don't think I will move."

In a world of political correctness, we have lost our sense of erotic power. We are so cautious about being sued, at taking a stand, or telling the truth, that we are becoming a homogenized culture of mediocrity. What do we stand for, what do we believe, where is our outrage? We turn our backs on presidential impropriety, yet watch as an eight-year-old boy is charged with sexual harassment for a playground kiss on the cheek. Erotic power calls us to take a stand.

In a recent address to the Harvard Law School Forum, Charlton Heston took on Time Warner for a CD they marketed called "Cop Killer." "At a stockholder's meeting," he said, "I stood and read every vicious, vulgar word of this cash cow. The room was a sea of shocked, frozen faces. The executives squirmed in their chairs and stared at their shoes. I was hated for it. Two months later, the CD was pulled from the market. Though I will never be offered another film by Warner or get a good review from *Time* magazine, disobedience means you must be willing to act."

The Right-Desire of power is in kinship with the disobedient spirit that protested the Vietnam War or tossed tea into the Boston Harbor. It is the vehicle that calls us to our feet to take a stand.

Attention

When closely inspected, one notices a nazuna in bloom under the hedge.
—BASHO, 17TH CENTURY

The contemporary Buddhist monk of fame, Thich Nhat Hanh, was invited to speak at the National Cathedral in Washington, D.C. In accordance with the tradition of the Episcopal Church, he was given the last position in the procession—the place of honor in this large, formal assembly. When the participants arrived at their designated places they turned, only to find the guest of honor just halfway down the aisle and still walking toward the chancel. Unaffected by the efficient pace of the military-like march, Thich Nhat Hanh was characteristically paying close attention to *every* step he was taking as the large gathering watched in silence.

Such a story becomes news to a culture that is built upon speed and efficiency. Whether commuting or computing, we want everything to move faster. But in so doing, we risk losing the details of each day that form the basis for the rest of our lives. If we are forever trying to live tomorrow before we have lived today, we miss the unique nuances of the present moment.

Our conscious mind blocks out much of the information that assaults our ongoing awareness. If this were not the case, we would experience sensory overload before 9:00 A.M. To survive, our prehistoric ancestors relied upon their capacity for paying attention; conversely, are we becoming less and less attentive because there is "too much, too fast?" I think so.

Recently, I entered my favorite coffeeshop and saw a woman whose name I did not know but whom I had greeted many times. On this day, noticing her new haircut, I added, "I like your haircut." "Thank you," she responded, then instantly punched the young man she was seated with and said, "See, *he* noticed!" Her beau might have benefited by paying closer attention to detail.

How many times in our early schooldays did we hear the classic command, "Pay attention!" It seems to be a common lament for teachers of wandering minds. Preacher and fifteenth-century mystic Meister Eckhart would often chastise his inattentive congregations, "Now listen to this, listen to me. I want you to pay attention." They probably regained focus for at least a minute—long enough for Eckhart to make some salient point.

Last year, I led a group of eighth graders on a trip to Grace Cathedral in San Francisco, for the purpose of walking the Labyrinth. Excited about participating in this first-time event, the group ran up the 80 stairs that led to the great edifice. Walking behind them I noticed, in the middle of this sea of concrete, an acorn proudly perched halfway up this great staircase. I stopped to look more closely at this unusual combination of seed and cement and thought, "Now that is optimism!" The image of that acorn attempting the near-impossible will forever remain in my mind whenever I need to believe in impossible things. If I, too, had run up the stairs, I most likely would have missed this important message.

The decision to pay attention to that which attracts us is the first step toward the giving of ourselves and creating spacious love. After we acknowledge that which attracts us, acceptance is the final step. Let us explore two components of attention: Presence and Patience.

Presence

Knowing how to be quiet when someone else is speaking is an important interior and exterior skill. A "quality listener" is able to allow another to speak without unnecessarily interrupting or interjecting. This is often difficult to practice in our fast-paced culture, one that feeds on speed.

"Quality Listening" is the name of a seminar I developed to teach people this most important leadership skill. It differs from most corporate training in that the entire morning of the day-long workshop is devoted to Practicing Presence. Seminar participants first engage in periods of silence. The participants are then ready to practice the interior skill of focusing on the needs of a speaker, rather than on their own stories or ego needs.

They discover the value of this attentiveness in the next exercise. Each participant is given a wooden matchstick. He or she observes its unique features for a full minute, and then returns it to a pile of nearly-identical matches. The participants are able to recognize and retrieve "their" matchsticks from the pile almost 100 percent of the time. This exercise demonstrates that when we learn to pay attention to otherwise-neglected details, we discover a world of information which is often hidden one layer below the surface. When managers stop multi-tasking long enough to turn their full attention to their employees, they become more than managers; they become mentors.

When we practice Presence and show up fully for another, what occurs in our relationships can be almost magical. Imagine a time when you were fully loved and cared for, with every need or want fulfilled. A birthday morning when you were kidnapped for the day and became the recipient of another's attention is now a lifetime memory. When someone close to you dropped everything in order to be available to you fully in a time of crisis, such Presence brought some form of healing. That is the magical power of Presence.

Practicing Presence requires the ability to suspend, temporarily, the needs of the ego that sings the relentless song, "What about me, what about me?" The temptation to tell a better story or give a more incredible example is based on our lack of personal security and the need to "best" another. Such behavior only serves as a billboard, advertising our need for personal enlightenment. When we allow speakers to tell *their* stories and walk their paths with them, we are creating a space for spacious love and communication at the deepest level.

As I stood in a group of business leaders at a luncheon recently, I noticed a man making the rounds, shaking hands and handing out his business cards. It appeared that his agenda was to become known quickly to as many people as possible. I was standing in a group with one of the corporate world's more prominent, successful, and "down-to-earth" CEOs. Our card-passing man introduced himself and asked the CEO his name; he received the information, but obviously did not recognize his face or name. When he asked the CEO what he did, the CEO responded, "Sales!" "I'm in sales, too," said the man. "Maybe we can get together for lunch and share some ideas." They exchanged cards, and when the CEO gave the man his card, he deposited it in his coat pocket without even glancing at it. Excusing himself, he quickly made his way to his next target area, having not a clue as to whom he had just spoken. The CEO displayed an ego that had no need to prove anything; he could allow the "glad-hander" to behave in a manner contrary to his own. Practicing Presence is not based upon personal need, but on a willingness to create a space where others can be who they authentically are.

84

The eyes and words of another always carry a unique experience about to happen. If we can remind ourselves that what is occurring will never, in the history of time, ever happen again in the same way, then we may be able to bring ourselves more fully to the experience. The moment I just spent writing the last sentence has passed and will not recur. Who I am and who you are has just changed. The Universe has expanded a bit more. Our bodies have gotten older and the earth has grown more tired. Every moment is a unique expression not to be taken for granted or ignored. Magic lies in the willingness to be present, to pay attention to the fullness of each moment.

PATIENCE

The ability to live in the fullness of each moment requires having the patience to remain present. Defined as quiet perseverance and even-tempered care, patience seems out of place in our fast-paced world, where to jump forward, finish someone else's thought, or "do it ourselves" is commonplace. How do we practice such a necessary component of the process of flow when speed is a way of life, "busyness" has become a status symbol, and waiting is something that we require only of our children?

Patience requires absence—the absence of judgment that aligns itself with self-absorption, along with the absence of inadequacy that is fueled by fear. The moment we begin to define efficiency or efficacy according to our own personal standards, we run the risk of losing any semblance of patience with those who do not fit our picture of perfection. Assessments that elicit from us such snap judgments as "idiot," "incompetent," or "jerk" are clear indicators that we have crossed over the line into the treacherous world of impatience.

In Your Patience is Your Soul

Seeing through the layers of an exterior persona, a wise pair of eyes perceives that our outer appearance is usually a reflection of what is occurring within. Personalized power, excessive materialism, or over-caregiving can be an over-compensation for feelings of inadequacy, just as perfectionism or over-achievement can be related to fear of failure. I confess to being intolerant of inefficiency, which is one of my greatest interior challenges.

Naturally, as a consultant, I find ways to improve the efficiency of sys-

85

tems or organizations. This talent is valued by business because it often means a more rewarding process for the employee as well as improved service for the customer. However, when *I* am the recipient of poor service, ill-conceived process, or a lack of common sense, I must breathe deeply before responding. Patience rears its head, looks me straight in the eye and asks me, "Jeffrey, what are you learning about *you?*"

To determine some kind of an answer, I must investigate the depths of my own emerging soul. Surrounding this interior self could be an external attitude of over-inflated, self-importance. This is a part of my persona; hence it becomes problematic. The extreme adoration by a mother who thought the sun rose and set with me may have laid the foundation for this unhealthy misperception; having a former career in which people would stand up the moment I, the celebrant of the liturgy, entered the worship space—this certainly was no help in tempering the attitude. The paradoxical task we all face is to hold in tension the acknowledgment that we "are not *that* important" with the awareness that we *are* uniquely, wonderful human beings who have our own place in the Universe's spotlight.

Further, I am also learning that such issues know no bounds. My intolerance of others reflects my intolerance of some aspects of myself. And I notice that the more intolerant I feel, the more intolerant my body becomes of substances that provoke the allergic reaction of wheezing and sneezing—a reminder of my soul's current state. Conversely, the more I am willing, without judgment, to understand the uniqueness of every person and experience each as a story in the process of development, the more my soul's true nature becomes prominent and my body performs at a higher level of efficiency.

Storytelling

Patience is the practice of remembering that each of us not only has a story, but that we *are* our stories as well. We are a collection of love stories and hate stories, myths and illusions, facts and fancies. Our stories have shaped us, just as we have shaped them. Human intercourse is a mixture of flesh and story; we introduce ourselves and we come to love the ones we meet through story. Thus we become natural storytellers, sharing the dramatic struggles that shape us, and communicating the collective wisdom of our experience. We must have the patience to regard and tell our stories as a way of charting our unfolding destiny. When we seek to know another

86

person, we listen to her or him with presence and patience, pondering the stories that have formed the one who speaks. These are not our stories; they belong to the character who carries as much pain and promise as we do. Two autobiographies mingled together are stories that can become etched in each other's hearts, fulfilling the hope of spacious love.

Sam and Ulele *are* a love story. At the age of two years, Ulele, the daughter of a Methodist Missionary, lost her mother, who died of malaria after giving birth to Ulele's brother Lionel. She and her brother were raised by various relatives in New Zealand, who took on the task for their traveling missionary brother as "their Christian duty." Breaking free from the constraint of this dutiful upbringing, Ulele left New Zealand to teach school in Fiji in 1941.

Sam was a 24-year-old First Lieutenant in the Navy making a survey of the harbor potential of the Fijian Islands. Having just escaped the bombing of Pearl Harbor, Sam was assigned to find possible new quarters for the American Navy. Instead, he found Ulele; ordered to "take care" of an officer's girlfriend during a bombing alert, Sam found the duty to be a life-long event. Sam, a dark-haired Muslim American sailor of Lebonese descent and Ulele, the strawberry-blonde daughter of a Christian evangelist, could not have been more different, yet their stories began to mingle the moment they met.

They fell in love but were separated by four more years of a world at war. Having stayed in touch by letter writing, Sam invited Ulele to San Francisco in 1945 for marriage and the hope for many years of a life lived together in fullness. The first post-war Trans-Pacific flight brought Ulele to America, to begin a shared story that would produce five children and a long life together. Their reverence and appreciation for each other is a story without words and serves as an example for all those who knew them and seek just such a devoted partnership and undying commitment in their own relationships.

Merrily Bronson is a story about learning how to die. As her widower husband Jim said, "She got to die when she was young. She did it energetically and she did it well. Her death made her life." Discovering her breast cancer in 1989, Merrily began the long, grim process known by countless women that included six months of chemotherapy and a radical mastectomy. With massive liver metastasis, Merrily entered an experimental program using genetically engineered antibodies to stop the voracious cancer.

In the winter of 1993, she earned a new identity. She did not die as predicted by her high-priced, well-known oncologists and surgeon. For 16 months, she improved and got stronger; she became more angel than human. Scuba diving with dolphins and climbing the Grand Tetons with her family, she returned to nearly total health. And then, for some unknown reason, the cancer returned.

Addressing an audience in San Francisco in 1994, Merrily said, "I was sitting out on our deck one day, feeling the pain of human suffering, and I thought, 'I don't want to fight my way back; it's just too painful out there.' And a thought popped into my mind that said, 'You don't need to *do* anything. You just need to be an entry point for love. That's all.' If I didn't have to do anything more than let love pour through me, it might just ripple out across the world. If I just aligned myself with love, that would make a difference. If all of us, not just people who are sick, lived our lives as if we were preparing for death, I think our lives would be much richer and more whole and our world would be a better place." The audience gave Merrily a standing ovation that lasted the entire time she said "Thank You," waved from the podium, and walked all the way to the back of the hotel ballroom.

Merrily's alignment with love transformed her into luminescence. And she began to live her death as she lived her life, touching the lives of all who knew her. How we die says a great deal about how we live. Perhaps her story will help shape our story of living and dying.

Practicing Patience—The Sharing of Stories

Family Love Stories ✖ Our families have been formed through a variety of love stories. Individuals from different paths and places have made their way toward each other to continue the development of a family line and legacy. Who are those people in your family, and what are their stories? Consider tracking the love stories of your grandparents or parents on videotape. Interview them for the "whole truth and nothing but the truth." What were the unique circumstances that brought them together? What are their stories of betrayed love, unrequited love, intimate love? What can you learn from their stories? How can their stories shape your story? Perhaps you are the one in your family line who will create the most complete love story yet. Can you be patient as your story evolves into your dream?

Family Hate Stories ❂ Tribal warfare was waged not only against threatening neighbors; it occurred within the tribe as well. Communities of love can also be communities with hate. It is the yin/yang, the dark/light, the matter/anti-matter, the thesis/antithesis of creative energy; it is the natural occurrence of opposites. We can track countless examples of stories in which the human ego's need for power negatively affects the quality of human relationships. It has happened within our own families. Where were the wars? Who never spoke to whom? Who was left out of the social gatherings? Who was the family "secret?" From the stories of hate we can learn as much about "how not to behave" as we can learn about "how to behave" from the stories of love. Can you, with patience and presence, listen to the stories that have made a contribution to your story? Can you relinquish judgment and view the tribal wars and pain of the past as a lesson not to recreate?

Stories of Triumph ❂ We are inspired by the examples of others who have triumphed over adversity and achieved excellence against all odds. We love "comeback" stories and we root for the underdog. As descendants of a Universe that was created from nothing, it is characteristically our way to "create something from nothing." Achievement helps form the psyche of the builder, the pioneer, and the explorer.

What stories of triumph and achievement are "soup for your soul" and inspire you along your path? What are your personal stories of triumph? What are the stories within your family, your industry, or your neighborhood? Stories live within everyone we know, just waiting to be revealed by the right question.

Stories of Failure ❂ I have learned more from my failures than my successes. In the Native American tradition, it would be said that my failures were "big medicine" for me. I have discovered that the most creative and successful organizations are those that allow for or even encourage risk-taking, with the possibility of failure. I once encouraged a start-up company to hold a "Friday-afternoon-failure party," in which everyone stood in a circle and with a glass of champagne in hand, toasted their most meaningful failure of the week. Then they shared what they learned from the experience. Finally, they all raised their glasses and toasted the learning-of-the-week.

What are the failures that have taught us meaningful life-lessons? What are the failures in our families, organizations, or personal relationships that make us wiser and deeper, and prepare us for similar challenges? Can we be patient with our own failures, seeing them as an integral part of our growth and just another step toward wisdom? Can we be patient with others who need to fail as a part of their learning and collecting of wisdom?

Personal Stories ✖ The gift of intimacy means being able to tell our stories to others who will hear us and love us because of who we are and who we are not. By embracing our true story, we make a commitment to honor our authentic selves. My own story involves growing up in a large family, knowing almost every person in our small, rural town of 3,500. Experiencing success in school and sports, I came to love the challenge of learning. I graduated with the same classmates I knew in kindergarten. Going away to a private, Ivy League college required a major adjustment. I left a large tribe, where I had been a "big frog in a little pond," to begin life in an unknown arena. As a middle-class, small-town high school graduate, I was insecure, frightened, and lonely, and struggled to compete with wealthy, prep school graduates. Although painful, those years were critical to the development of my current story.

Can you, with patience, look back over the steps completed thus far, and look forward to the ongoing journey? Can you appreciate the value of your evolution and look, with wonder, upon the many factors contributing to your uniqueness?

Tribal Stories ✖ In South Africa, a tradition called "Endaba" gives tribal members the opportunity to sit together and speak whenever, and for as long as, they want. Almost every indigenous people has some formalized custom for communication that holds the community together like a social glue. It gives everyone a sense of belonging to a common heritage.

Likewise, every collection of people who work or live together has tribal stories. Employees of one San Francisco construction company that I work with were seeking the best way to let potential clients know who they were and what their presence meant to the city. I led them in a process by which they shared stories they had heard and other stories that they had created. This resulted in ten key stories that readily unveiled their company's history and the purpose behind their work. Selling themselves to others became much easier through the telling of these stories.

What are the historical beginnings that reveal your uniqueness? Who were the primary characters and what were their visions? How have others joined this dream to achieve success? When we are willing to listen to the features of tribal stories, we honor the past and the work of others that has made their vision a reality.

Waiting

Waiting is an integral component of patience. We do not do it well. Although we consistently tell our children, "Wait," adults have short fuses when issued the same command. Our indignance rises to the surface as if our agenda were the most important factor in the equation of time. Traffic jams become a personal issue, an hour-long wait for a restaurant table is considered "ridiculous" and delayed flights are a cosmic plot to undermine our time management. However, if we can learn to wait, we discover meaning in whatever develops and teachers we may not have noticed. Just as a conscious person has the ability to wait for a stuttering person to complete a sentence, we can all learn to wait while another story unfolds, one scene at a time, without our assistance.

Sonia's Story

Several years ago I arrived at a doctor's appointment, only to be told that my physician had an emergency and I would be seen by another doctor within an hour's time. Impatience made itself known because of the many things I had hoped to accomplish that day, but I chose to wait and use the time to read the material I had brought with me. One hour and ten minutes later, I was called into the examination room. Having never met this particular physician, I asked questions about his particular story through normal conversation. By the end of the routine examination, I had discovered that he attended a university with someone with whom I had lost contact ten years ago. He, too, had known her, but also had lost contact. I had an intuitive sense that she was in trouble and we needed to find her. Together, we began the pursuit of tracking her down through the university filing system. Three weeks later, we made contact with her and discovered her sounding clinically depressed and suicidal. I flew to Missouri and drove two hours to where she was living. Two hours later, she was hospitalized for treatment and now is on her way to living a balanced and fulfilling life. What were the advantages of waiting one hour and ten minutes? Many!

Authors know that it is essential to "wait" when the flow of words and ideas is not forthcoming. Time has meaning, and in the waiting, new material is forming and old ideas are maturing. If I had published this work two years ago when the project began, it would be far different from its current state. Nor would it be the same next year. That is the beauty of quantum flow: it is a constant process of evolution and change. It is like the weather in Chicago—if you don't like it, wait a few minutes and it will change.

Our need for instant gratification has consumed our ability to wait. We have lost touch with our agrarian roots, when we naturally planted seeds, waited, and reaped the harvest, thus benefiting from attending the growth process. When we can learn to wait without frustration, exasperation or judgement, then we have begun to walk the path of true patience and are primed for the final component of the holy trinity of spacious love: acceptance.

Acceptance

We come to love, not by finding the perfect person, but by learning to see an imperfect person perfectly. —SAM KEEN

One of life's greatest pleasures is to be "wholly known and wholly loved." When we sit in the presence of someone who accepts us for who we are, just as we are, we become our most beautiful self. We are the recipients of one of humankind's greatest attributes, compassion. Compassion is our link with our soul—the closest expression of the Divine that we can manufacture. From the Latin, *pati cum*, compassion means we "suffer with" the one who is different, who is wounded, who is contrary. Compassion is not compatible with comparison. The moment we compare, we yield compassion. Although we each want to be loved just as we are, without being judged by another, we still can judge others just as we wish *not* to be judged. The following is a story of compassion where two hearts met and understood—from chaplain intern Emily Gutherie, who saw the light hidden inside a dark spirit, and Ms. Cherry, the one who hid the light from everyone but Emily.

The Story of Ms. Cherry (as told by Emily Gutherie)

During the summer of 1994, I spent 12 weeks at the St. Elizabeth's Campus of the District of Columbia Mental Health Division, otherwise known as "St. E's." The Administrators of the Clinical Pastoral Education Program assigned me to be "Summer Chaplain" to three wards: 7b, which housed the former

criminally insane; 9a, a long-term care; and the geriatric ward at the acute hospital. 7bWard imprisoned a blind gentleman (whose crime was acute dependency) and another character who became obsessed with me and the constitutionality of my presence on the ward—all in an effort not to talk about the state of his soul after he brutally murdered his mother. The former offered his Braille version of Luke's Gospel; the latter drew inverted crosses on my notebooks. Both sought me regularly. Ward 9a was home to one Adam, two Jesuses and one Almighty.

Surprisingly, it was the geriatric ward that eventually taught me the most that summer. These patients were hospitalized for short, involuntary visits that often extended into many weeks as staff scrambled to find nursing homes willing to take the destitute, who have a tendency to shout or run naked through the hallways.

Ms. Cherry trailed me from my first day, literally like a shadowy madwoman. I have no idea how old she was, perhaps 70. She had mocha skin and gray hair that resembled those famous pictures of Einstein. I never saw her wear shoes or utter an intelligible sentence. On the first day I visited the acute geriatric ward, Ms. Cherry tore off her clothes in the middle of the room to a chorus of staff-member protests: "Put those clothes on this minute, Ms. Cherry, or you can forget about a snack. Will somebody PLEASE get Ms. Cherry a robe? She's buck naked again in the common room!"

I think it was day four when she began hiding behind corners in order to scream in my ear when I walked by. She loved how I jumped, and when she discovered that I could laugh with her afterwards, I was in. With some of the patients I talked, with others I listened, or consulted; with Ms. Cherry however, I played. The nurses clucked, "Don't pay no mind to Cherry, that woman is GONE!" Her chart read simply, "Dementia," no personal history, a few notes about "decompensation," and behaviors requiring restraints.

Several weeks into the program I noticed that often, while I was visiting a certain patient, Ms. Cherry suddenly would appear next to me, hands folded, head cocked, eyes wild. She would just stare at me and "pretend" to have a conversation with me. She watched what the others did, and held the pose for two or three minutes before tearing off or stealing chocolate milk from the food tray.

I don't remember if I always paused and included her in the conversation, but I know I did on several occasions. She never responded. Once, when I was deep in conversation with a patient over biblical trivia, Ms. Cherry started her *striptease in the middle of the common room. Wondering what she was trying to communicate, I told her that, although she looked beautiful, it was probably more dignified and less disturbing to others if she kept her clothes on. She responded by "giving me the eye" and departing to the TV wing. I reflected on how naïve I was to try to engage this woman in normal conversation.*

On my last day as summer chaplain, I said goodbye to each patient on the acute geriatric ward, some of whom I had grown to love deeply. For others, I was just a face. As I made my way toward Ms. Cherry, she was sitting with her head on the table. I knelt next to her, took her hand and explained to her that this was my last day. I told her that I had to go back to school but that I had really enjoyed knowing her. I told her what I most appreciated about her was her sense of humor.

In a moment that is burnt into my memory forever, she lifted her head, looked into my eyes, and carefully whispered, "Thank you." That moment crystallized my understanding of the power of the soul and the presence of God, even when the body and mind seem to be gone. Ms. Cherry will forever serve as an example of what can happen when we accept one another "just as we are."

The Balance Practice: Dancing

> *Learn to recognize the counterfeit coins*
> *That may buy you just a moment of pleasure*
> *But then drag you for days*
> *Like a broken man*
> *Behind a farting camel*
>
> *And from the most insignificant movements*
> *Of your own holy body*
> *Now, sweet one,*
> *Be wise.*
> *Cast all your votes for Dancing!*
>
> —HAFIZ

I define dancing as "the ultimate sacrifice of human flesh; the undulating, stretching, and exposing of raw spirit underneath the callused skin covering that often *over-protects* us from necessary vulnerability." A simpler expression might be, "Get down and Boogie!" Get down into what? Into the deepest and most creative part of who we are—our soul.

Relationships require the fluidity of give-and-take, initiation and re-

94

sponse; speaking and hearing; touching and being touched; seeing and being seen; believing and being believed; trusting and being trusted; pushing out, pulling back. It's all a sacred dance— touch-step, touch-step, and 1-2-3-4, 1-2-3-4, again . . .

Rigor mortis is the stiffness of the dead body. For many, it seems also to be a body posture that can be experienced in a vertical position. Ancient wisdom teaches the simple fact, "If you can walk, you can dance," yet most do not believe it. Although the same muscle coordination is required, the moment the music is on and the invitation to dance is issued, the body descends into the ballroom grave. Relationships that dance—that risk foolishness, embarrassment, and God forbid, *vulnerability*—are the ones that deepen and flourish.

Just as the body needs to laugh, the spirit needs to dance. If you think about it, dancing is no less exposing. When we laugh, we open our mouths as wide as possible, exposing all our dental history and occasionally make a raucous sound from the bowel area. We can drool, cry, snort, wheeze, gasp, honk, or spit, but does that stop us? NOOOOO! Dancing, by comparison, is so civilized: no drooling or spiting; hardly a tear or snort, just moving the body parts in different directions—simultaneously. Maybe that is the problem. We are so committed to the staid structure of unified movement and looking "together" that we are fearful of appearing disintegrated.

Consider your own dance history; you may have had some traumatic beginnings. The fourth-grade formal dance class at the local club may have put you into a pretty party dress or a pair of tails that made you look wonderful on the outside but created much interior tension. The young boys touch was partially insulated through the invention of white gloves. Not only did it protect the young male warrior from *touching a girl*; it protected the young maiden from the profusely sweaty hands of the nervous boy.

Let us move forward to the Junior High Dance—short boys on one side of the gym and much taller girls in the bathroom. Senior High Dance— slightly taller boys on one side of the gym and tall girls in the bathroom. Progress! If fast dancing did occur, girls usually danced with girls while boys watched. SLOW DANCE! Everybody's now on the floor. Directions! Wrap your arms around each other in order to feel as many maturing body parts as possible, and then rock back and forth to the mantra: "DO NOT MOVE THE FEET." College—Drink enough beer so that you won't feel foolish (of course, a lot of beer never made any of us *look* foolish) and then find the young woman from math class that you have been staring at all semester, and ask her for a dance. When she refuses, you return to drink more beer. When your favorite song comes on, you cast away all inhibition and rush to the dance floor alone and just move—acting at least, like you are dancing with someone. When Chuck, the left-defensive tackle who is dancing next to you with his girlfriend, tells you to move out of his space and to stop facing him as if you were dancing with him, you go home, having had enough for one night.

In spite of these beginnings, dance is what our bodies want to do. It is the expression of the higher self through the physical limbs, responding to billions of electrical impulses that rush through nerve endings with the message: let go, play, have fun, rock, be foolish, "CAST ALL YOUR VOTES FOR DANCING." Once my friend Laura and I were on a trip when our favorite song came on the radio. Pulling the car over to the emergency area (and this *was* an emergency) on the side of the road, in full view of all driving by—we danced. A similar emergency arose one morning at 5:00 A.M. on the way back from Starbuck's Coffee. One of my all-time favorite songs started to play. Inspired by a great night's sleep and four shots of espresso, I needed—not wanted, but *needed*—to dance. Since Bear was the only one with me, I waited until we reached the front of our home and then invited my "date" to dance. Rising up on his two back legs with his front legs around me, he willingly cast aside all his dog inhibition, and we danced.

The Twelve-Step Program

Start Alone:

1. Make a list of all the people you have stepped on or harmed in any way; make direct amends and promise that you will return with new abilities and attitudes.
2. When you know that you will have some time alone, rent some dance movies (*Flashdance, Lets' Dance, Shall We Dance?, Saturday Night Fever*, any Gene Kelly or Fred Astaire films), sit behind closed doors and invite inspiration to join you.
3. Turn on some loud music, turn off all the lights, close your eyes and just let your body move without judging yourself about how you look.

4. Get an outfit—some tight polyester pants are a must—lock all the doors and pull the shades. Now turn on some lighting, keep your eyes open and start dancing to your favorite tunes in front of the mirror. Convince yourself that you look really cool.
5. Invent some moves and practice them enough so they will look as natural as two 40-pound pigs wrestling in a pillowcase, when all eyes are upon you.

In Public:

6. Wait until the music starts (Do not start dancing before the music starts.)
7. Move quietly toward the floor and find a corner where there is enough space to flail your arms and legs without injuring anyone.
8. Make a decision to turn your will and your life over to the care of God as you understand Her.
9. Rock 'n' Roll.
10. When you realize that you have survived the first song, go for a few more. Make it look as if you are actually dancing with someone by putting your arms around your partner's waist or kissing him or her softly on the neck.
11. Pick yourself up off the floor and wipe the blood from your nose.
12. Having realized that as a result of these steps you are now a dancer, carry this message to all non-dancers and practice these steps while waiting in line at the Post Office. *"Dance as if nobody is watching."*

Weaving the Seamless Fabric

The creation of space is an art necessary for creating lasting relationships. When we create space around us, for us, between us and within us, we prepare for inviting the sacred to reside within that space and begin the holy work of communion. We create space all the time and don't realize it. We create space each night between the covers as a sanctuary for safe rest, renewal and romance. As pioneers once sought the open space of the expansive West for their unbridled vision, we too, intuitively seek an openness in relationship that makes room for our dreams and for the totality of our unique nature. When we consider space to be spherical as opposed to linear, we open the door to immense possibilities that can be as large as the Universe. By contrast, limited space will suffocate us and contribute to the slow process of soul death.

Humphrey the Whale was a visitor to the San Francisco Bay Area in 1984. Although whales are most common to western waters, Humphrey was an adventurous grey whale that strayed from the vast playground of the Pacific Ocean into the confines of the San Francisco Bay. Newscasters followed Humphrey's daily escapades and the Bay area became mesmerized by its journey. Stopping traffic on the Golden Gate Bridge as Humphrey played in the bay waters, the whale seemed content with its new digs. But as it traveled north into the shallower waters of the Delta, Humphrey's life became endangered. A massive effort began to turn it around and encourage the whale back to sea. Weeks passed as Humphrey's life became more threatened. Eventually, it wisely turned and began the journey back to the space where it could thrive. Like the great whale, we are meant to live in territories that are wide and deep. The moment we are confined to a space that is narrow and shallow, our souls begin to die. We thrive upon the spacious love of unlimited space and the gift of acceptance.

When we create an inner space for love, we create a place for trust, honor and reverence. These energies become a wondrous alchemy that reminds us of the sacred nature of life and how we can live a life fully expressed. From the context of such a full experience, we build a foundation for all that will be created in our outer world of symbols and cities. As our outsides reflect our insides, we create what we are. Who we are then, is a most important work. It is *the work* within our work, it is *the contribution* to relationships, and it is *the primary focus* of self-care. We are a seamless fabric, a weave of the intricate threads of meaning and purpose.

CIRCLE THREE

Work

Weaving the Seamless Fabric of Passion, Purpose and Gifts

When our eyes see our hands doing the work of our hearts, the circle of creation is completed inside us, the doors of our souls fly open and love steps forth to heal everything in sight. —MICHAEL BRIDGE

We Are Our Work

I do not believe that we have arrived on this planet for the sole purpose of being in a lifelong relationship, nor for the purpose of creating children. While each of those can be a wonderful aspect of the life-journey, they are not the ultimate reason that we are here. If you find this thought disturbing, consider this alternative: *We are here to discover the ways in which we can serve the common good through the gifts we have been given.* When we discover ways to bring healing to the needs of the world, we begin to enjoy a fullness of life that is reflected in our work. When our work is our reason for being—it becomes our bliss, our joy, our heart's passion, our art, our legacy, and our gift to the world.

Author and contemplative monk Thomas Merton said, "If you want to know who I am, don't ask me where I live or what I like to eat, or how I comb my hair. Ask what I am living for and push me on it." Merton knew that his work was a reflection of who he was and his reason for living; that how he acted determined the quality of the gift he created for the benefit of humankind. If he did not do his best, he wanted to be challenged to maximize his potential. He *was* his work, and he wanted to leave a legacy that reflected who he was in his entirety.

99

Management studies prove that 82 percent of the work-climate quality is determined by the manager's individual behavior. A grumbling manager is no different than a grumbling mate or parent who sours the home climate; we are all affected by the moods and behaviors of persons with authority. And if we are the source of any such negativity, it is our job to purge those issues fueling that negativity. In so doing, we "become our work."

The people of the Appalachian Mountains have a phrase for greeting one another that is much more meaningful than the banal, "Hi, how are you?" greeting common to our culture. After a friendly salutation they ask, "What's workin' ya?"—which means, "What issues are the driving force behind your thoughts, feelings, and actions?" Their simple wisdom gets to the heart of the reality that we are the sum total of our experience, that whatever is going on inside of us affects or drives our behavior. Insecurity can drive overcompensation; fear of intimacy can create protected vulnerability; and the experience of abuse can be the driving force behind retaliation or powerless submission. On the positive side of this formula, trust supports a willingness to take risks, while compassion supports the authentic use of power.

Another aspect of "being our work" is the unification of our multiple roles. Although all of us have different roles that we fill, life-balance requires that we be authentically the same person within each of those roles. The compassion and understanding required for good parenting is no different than the qualities needed to manage a productive work environment. The commitment to quality and excellence in industry is the same commitment that contributes to a healthy and balanced home life or a finely tuned body. *Living simultaneously* is not a compartmentalization of our work and personal lives, but a process that involves all things, all of the time.

How we do anything is how we do everything.

Living as closely in accordance with our authentic selves as we can is the challenge of life-balance. At the core of our being, each of us has an authentic and wonderful self that experiences pleasure and sorrow, hope and despair, love and fear. If we present a persona to the outer world that is not consistent with the workings of our inner core, we are not living authentically.

The Russian philosopher George Gurdjieff taught about the two worlds of personality and essence: When our personality is a clear reflection of our essence, (our most authentic self), we experience the balance of the inner and outer worlds.

Who we are on the inside is who we bring to our work every day. If we put on masks to hide our interior lives, we will not know the true benefits of authenticity. Our work relationships can become more rich with the same kind of growing intimacy we experience in our personal relationships.

One of the factors that can make our work more satisfying is the love from self and others that sustains us. We cannot come to work and check our hearts at the door; we cannot live in different worlds as two different people. We are quantum people— fully connected to all things, and all things a part of us. And if we are to understand fully the meaning of work, we must first do the inner work of knowing ourselves and "what is working us." This is the essential first step toward understanding the theme, "we are our work."

Bringing the Whole Self to Work

As we suggested in Circle One, Self Care, no one aspect of body, mind or spirit functions wholly without the other; the mind without the body becomes a vision without limbs and requires the work of others to create the dream. The body without the expansiveness of the mind becomes merely another object hurtling through space, without direction. And the passion of the soul, without the mind's commitment or the body's execution, becomes a dream, endlessly awaiting rebirth so that the life-purpose can be fulfilled. When these three elements become the threads of life woven together, they create one seamless tapestry; and the world's eye cannot distinguish where one life-element begins and another ends.

Work is of the Soul

Without work, all life goes rotten but when work is soulless, life stifles and dies.
—ALBERT CAMUS

In my work with senior executives, I discovered one of their most compelling needs: usually toward the end of their careers, they realize that contributing and making a difference through their work is more important than anything else. This becomes most important as they fulfill the calling of the soul, which is to make more than a living—it is to make a difference. Although our relationships are our heart's passion and the care of our selves is not negotiable, not to matter and to make no contribution to the world is spiritual death. Making a difference gives meaning to our lives and, directly or inadvertently, touches the lives of others. When we discover passion and purpose in our work, it becomes the road to a life fully expressed. Such a life calls us to leadership, to betterment. This is soul-work.

When our jobs are at odds with our core values and beliefs, we slowly spiral downward toward spiritual death. Poet David Whyte aptly described this plight when he wrote: "The soul is constantly trying to belong in ways that are not necessarily good for the average career." When we are courageous enough to venture into the heart of the soul, we often discover a calling to something quite different from what we expected.

Although my leadership-development company is retained by companies to "fix" managers and leaders who have behavioral issues, we often discover that after coaching, a large percentage leave their jobs and follow their hearts. As one client recently said, "I am tired of greed and the pursuit of power. It is meaningless." He left his executive position to obtain a teaching credential. He now teaches eighth grade at an urban school, and "has never felt more fully alive."

This section will investigate the meaning of the phrase "we are our work," and probe the reality that our jobs may *not* be our work. We will explore how our work becomes a lasting legacy when passion, purpose, and our individual gifts meet the needs of the world.

Catherine

Let me introduce you to Catherine, a story-book character I created as an example of the person who lives within the potential of us all. She serves as such a good example of the seamless tapestry that all of us desire, that three readers of a previous version of this book in which she was presented as a "real person", asked me if they could meet her! I had to inform them that she exists only within their own potential.

A partner in a nearby city's largest law firm, she is a woman in her late sixties who thrives in a life lived simultaneously. When Catherine walks into a room, there is an air of reverence approaching awe surrounding her fit and erect body. Her keen mind is so quick and well-informed that it is common for others to take notes when she speaks. The openness of her thoughts embraces change as a welcome guest, since her thinking cannot be contained within any single parameter. When approached with a risky, yet reasonable idea, her natural response is likely to be, "Let's do it!" This assures the visionary not only of her support, but of her ongoing presence as well. Compassion is also evident in her voice and in her work. When in her company, you feel as if you are the most important person in the world; she listens to you and she observes you. She is a woman of substance and of extraordinary power.

What makes Catherine this seamless tapestry, this perfect blend of mind, body, and spirit? What is the basis for such stability and life-fullness? Is this an act she performs for the critical eye of the world, or is it the picture of her authentic self? I discovered that her secret formula resides in the power of a song she sings, which she has given me permission to share with you.

My Body's Your Temple

VERSE ONE: *My body is a temple of the Divine, where the spirit of creation resides. It is a sacred object that has been given to my care.*

This is how Catherine's song begins each day. Says Catherine, "I don't feel a bit apologetic for beginning with what the Divine has given me. It is a part of my work, and if I don't start with caring for the way I feel, then my mind and spirit are sluggish. Nourishing the body is the foundation for all else that follows."

Her routine is very focused and intentional. She rises at 4:45 A.M. and begins each day with silence, stretching, and yoga. She eats a light breakfast consisting of a blended shake with all the necessary vitamins and minerals. Three days per week, on her way to work, she stops off at the gym for an hour of light weight training, aerobics, or swimming. Her diet consists of protein, fresh vegetables and fruit with plenty of water and adequate carbohydrates. She loves her morning coffee and enjoys two glasses of a wonderful Merlot at the day's end. While she enjoys desserts and pasta, she rarely eats food with empty calories. She is not perfect, but she is very healthy.

The concept of the body as a temple of the Divine is an ancient one. Remembering that concept allows us to *re-member* our physical structure in a new way. Such attention can evoke enormous strength, as we learn to tap an unlimited resource of power that can re-create our bodies countless times. Catherine suffered from a mild stroke ten years ago. Partially paralyzed for one year, she was determined to re-define her body in a fresh way. Her daily commitment to ultimate health resulted in her complete recovery and her belief that *the body is a temple of the Divine where the spirit of creation resides.*

Caring for the Mind

VERSE TWO: *My mind is a channel for wisdom. Imagination is evidence of the Divine. May your thoughts be my thoughts.*

This is how Catherine's song continues. She is an insatiable reader, and her reading list knows no limits. Always expanding the parameters of her mind, she makes time each day to read, whether at work or at home. "When my mind is stimulated by the notion of something new, I realize that I am experiencing the intersection of my thoughts and divine thoughts. I become energetic and productive. Learning is a pathway to my energy and a sacred event," she says. To ensure this sacred interaction, Catherine includes a "reading morning" each week, despite her demanding schedule. "It's all a matter of choosing to stay home, saying no to the pressure that comes from what appears to be such an outrageous action, and feeding my mind with what I need to know. My clients certainly understand, even if my partners don't."

Although in her late sixties, she began taking piano lessons last year. She is currently learning to scuba dive, and, for next year, has set her sights on a private pilot's license. "Every encounter with learning is an opportunity to experience the Divine at work," she says. "People are my teachers and experience is my lesson." This attitude permeates her work; she serves as a mentor to all of her staff at their request. There are no hours kept and no annual performance evaluations. Her leadership is built upon trust and ongoing interaction with each member of her staff.

A member of the legal profession for over 30 years, Catherine remains on the cutting-edge of ways to reinvent work. Most of her staff have worked with her for over 15 years. She invented "off-sites" for staff once each quarter, for what she refers to as "days away." "This is a time for building the team," reports Catherine, "finding out how my associates are doing in their personal lives, asking for feedback about how I am doing from their perspective and what we all can do to create a healthier place to work. This is so simple and yet it still makes the statement, 'Your thoughts matter to me because they are evidence of the Divine.'"

Feeding the Soul

VERSE THREE: *I am not apart from anything. I am in You and You are in me. Spirit makes us one.*

Catherine has a marvelous formula for keeping a unified balance: earning, learning and serving. "Although earning is fun and learning is divine, serving others is the best way I remain connected to the other two aspects, and it keeps me true to my life purpose. It also is the greatest source of my strength." Catherine's way of serving knows no bounds. She is a volunteer in soup kitchens, a member of a nonprofit foundation, a contributor of 20 percent of her income to charity, a wonderful mother of two, and a creative grandmother of four. She is a woman of serving spirit, and when you approach her, she welcomes you into her presence just with the look in her eyes. Time does not rule her spirit, but instead is her humble servant. She decides how and what she does with the time allotted her, not the reverse.

Catherine's soul is fed by her work because what she values is what she lives; there is no inconsistency. Catherine is an example of "quantum work"—she is a part of everything and everything is a part of her. Especially important to her process is the pain she has experienced, as well as the failures she has known. She endured the trauma of her parents' alcoholism and their desperate addiction. She lost her husband at an early age, never again to find the love of a soul mate. She failed at two of her own businesses and teetered at the brink of financial disaster for five years. Yet through all this she never lost hope or her vision of what life could be like. She embraced pain and frustration, and became a bigger and deeper soul as a result of their presence.

That the success of her life is also greater relates to her unwillingness to compartmentalize her time, to divide her life as if it were a pie. Instead, she lives simultaneously, drawing upon all aspects of life and flowing with a divine rhythm. She moves steadily like a stream that flows around barriers, and cuts a path that is both deep and lasting. A turbulence akin to white water can be evident, yet just below its surface is a deep and abiding calm. She knows where she is going and follows a path that returns to her origin, the limitless power of her internal sea.

Our Job May Not Be Our Work

Jobs are important. Thirteen years ago, I had no job and knew well the fear that accompanied such a circumstance. I have also experienced the deep and bitter frustration of others who had no way of providing for their basic needs. While leading a large group of American youth in a work project in Ireland almost two decades ago, I spoke with angry Irish youths who believed they had virtually no prospects for work in their entire lifetime, and were therefore relegated to a "life on the dole." Aging business executives who are "let go," replaced by younger and less-experienced individuals feel the pain associated with being jobless. The millions of homeless in America—many with college degrees—feel a hopelessness about getting off the street. Creating enough jobs for the world's exploding population is one of humankind's biggest challenges, and an essential first step toward meeting humanity's basic needs.

When we are fortunate enough to have a job that meets the our basic needs, it allows us the luxury to hold the concept that *our job may not be our work.* Many people spend long hours each day in efforts that require their time and energy, but do not feed their soul. This is why they are unhappy in their jobs; their jobs do not relate to their work. Their jobs are too small for their spirits, and *their souls are constantly trying to belong in ways that are not necessarily good for the average career.* However, there are times when this is a transitory stage that must continue in order for one to meet life's basic needs.

We can feel confident that the soul will not let us remain forever in something that does not feed our internal life. People often ask, "Am I just supposed to leave my job to follow my passion?" Wise counsel suggests that unless you have financial security, an unfailing belief in your abilities or no choice at all, it is best to begin the process of discovering one's work while working within any job. *A disturbing thing about the soul is that it would rather fail in its own life than succeed in someone else's.* When constrained, the soul will eventually break free and begin the pursuit of its true path. That may be the first step in discovering "our work."

A young woman working for a fast-paced software company discovered that the company's values were clearly inconsistent with her own. She felt herself grow more tired and removed with each passing month. After she examined the values of the corporation, she discovered the misalignment—her soul was too big for her job. She left the company, took the $5,000 she had saved and toured the world alone for six months, exploring her passion for travel. Now she is in the process of seeking a job elsewhere that is more consistent with her values, one that will afford her the opportunity to travel and work simultaneously.

I am blessed by having a job that is my work. Every day, I get to practice my art and do what I love most—but I had to create it. Ten years ago, I knew that my work related to using creative means to help others tap their own unlimited potential. However, that work had no form; I had to create a job that reflected what I valued. Teaching, speaking, writing, and the individual coaching of others today affords me a way to express my work. With that heartfelt expression comes not only great satisfaction in knowing that I make a difference in the lives of some, but can also earn an income that cares for my basic needs as well. Can you do this? I believe you can, but first consider this: your work may not be far from your reach. It may, in fact, be within your existing job.

Discovering Your Work Within Your Job

Gordon hated his job. After years of doing the same thing, he felt as though he were dying on the inside. Everything was routine and nothing seemed new, and he felt that he was collecting a paycheck just for "showing up." It was during one of our Eagle Leadership Seminars that he came to a new understanding: he discovered that what he loved best was coaching others toward personal growth within their jobs. He relished the time he spent with his employees, guiding them toward personal achievement and satisfaction. Even though his own work was tedious to endure, he discovered the simple fact that ultimately his job provided the environment for doing what he loved most. When he adjusted his perspective, his job became the vehicle for his work. Today—within the same job—he executes his own tasks more efficiently, in order to make more time for doing what he truly loves.

Countless businesspeople are in their jobs not because of passion or a clear sense of purpose, but because they believe they need their jobs to live. Working simply to live can become a death spiral, claiming the soul early on in one's life. The phrase "it's just a job" itself signifies resignation. In the town where I grew up, I watched mill workers go to work each day to the sound of a siren. Ten-hour shifts must have been the norm, because the siren captured them at 8 A.M., not to release them until 6 P.M. If they were "lucky," overtime work earned them "time-and-a-half" pay, and the money thereby accumulated, affording them a variety of ways to forget the hard work they endured. And so the downward spiral continued.

As radical as this may sound, work is *not* exclusively for the purpose of making money. Certainly, money is a wonderful tool with which to meet our basic needs, but beyond that it brings little satisfaction —it is not a means to an end. What people want most is to discover that they make a difference, and that their work is their art.

Work as Art

When our work is the deepest expression of who we are, we are our work. It becomes not only our lifestyle, but our own personal art form. Unfortunately, the artist residing within each of us is often buried at the deepest level of our psyche. Most people do not believe they have the capacity for art because they have been taught something to the contrary. Often, some damaging childhood experience leaves us with the perception that we cannot create, draw, paint, sing, dance or sculpt. But we can—and we can do *more* than that. We can build relationships, invent new ways to behave, form new communities, fashion new designs, compose new songs to ourselves, fabricate new dreams, manufacture better products, or even construct a new world. We are serving our creative passion all the time, and when we acknowledge this process of creating, something begins to stir deep within us. When our soul becomes enlivened, our passion emerges, and we align ourselves with the creative forces of the Universe as co-creators.

My eldest sister, Barbara Barden is a passionate artist. She does not paint, sculpt or play a musical instrument, yet her passion makes her life her art. Each week she sends herself flowers with a note that says, *To Barbara: Just because you're you.* She receives the flowers at the door with a squeal of delight, as if surprised by a gift from a secret lover. Her baking and cooking are each testaments to her passion for food, and the warmth of her home reflects her passion for hospitality. Her humor and laughter attest to her love for life and Barbara's creative thinking flows effortlessly, as if she has tapped into a Divine resource for ideas.

Classic burnout is not the result of doing too much, but rather of doing too much of what we do not want to do. I have quoted poet David Whyte several times in this circle. He seems to have grasped the concept that work relates to the soul of the artist. However, he had to discover this wisdom through his own life-experience. After working in a traditional job that did not allow him to devote enough time to his passion for reading and writing poetry, he sought the advice of his mentor, Brother David Steindal-Rasdt. "What is the antidote for burnout?" he asked. Brother David responded, "It is not rest that will relieve you of burnout. Instead, the antidote for burnout is the rediscovery of your passion, and following it." Whyte did just that, and has contributed much to a hungry world through his artistic passion—poetry.

Executive coaches are often retained to work with people who have some kind of performance or attitude problem. It usually becomes clear that these attitude and performance problems stem from the fact that people are "dying the slow death" of maintaining a career path rather than expressing their art. Their passion is gone, and instead of *living simultaneously*, they have joined the ranks of the "living dead."

Falling in love is one of those passionate events that we all seek and cherish. It is a time of flowing endorphins, energy, excitement, hopefulness and creativity. That euphoric feeling of lightness and playfulness comes from the same source that inspires the entrepreneur within each of us to feel much the same way about a new idea or business venture. We *can* experience the same Divine source of all creative love, both in relationships and in our work. Rediscovering or renewing our passion at work is the key, not only to our success, but also, to our soul's well-being.

Think of our work as a sacred triangle of passion, purpose, and gifts. When we discover our passion and are clear that our ultimate purpose is to give to others through the use of the gifts we have been given—that is when the magic of art begins and our work becomes a gift to the world. It is also through this process that we discover our calling. Author Frederick Buechner describes it this way: "To find our calling is to find the intersection between the deep gladness of our hearts and the world's deep hunger."

Because we are a people of deep and profound hunger, the world will respond to the deep gladness of our hearts. There is just as much hunger in the training rooms of corporations as on the streets of our cities. It does not matter whether it is the hunger of those who do not have enough or if it is the search for wholeness with which to heal the fractured lives of those who are choking from too much: we are all hungry and in need of the gift of each other's passion, purpose, and gifts.

⊠ PASSION FOR WORK

Something led you to your present job: there was a spark of some kind that promised you opportunity and fulfillment. There is also a reason that you are doing the work that you are presently doing. What was it that made your heart leap when you thought about your new "work"? What important life-lesson are you learning? Who is there that serves as your teacher? These factors are the key to finding the elements of your passion. Work is the ultimate expression of the soul, and therefore reflects the most important aspect.

So often, we can move through life forgetful of passion's power and deadened to its familiarity. After pondering the questions below, if you discover that your passion is slowly dying, it is imperative that you make a move. Remembering what passion feels like is a necessary part of that redirection.

Whenever I need passion's strength, I intentionally try to evoke the memory of selected events that awaken that feeling of passion. Memories of passion become a "heart song" that renews us and reminds us that we are meant to love and to feel deeply.

One of my own personal selected memories is an event that occurred when my two daughters were four and seven years of age. Entering the front door of my house at day's end, I heard their mother call to them, "Girls, Daddy's home." I looked down the hallway toward their bedroom as they ran out to greet me. In pink matching dresses, with black patent-leather shoes and their hair pigtailed, they began racing toward me shouting, "Daddy, Daddy!" Almost as if in slow motion, I dropped to my knees with my arms outstretched, watching them run toward me. Shoes clacking along the wooden floor and their pigtails bobbing from their forward motion, they ran into my arms, kissing and embracing me by the neck. I felt uplifted, illuminated, grateful, peaceful, and powerful—all at the same time. It was a moment of complete joy.

If we are able to identify which aspects of our job provide a response of similar feeling, we are on the path toward discovering our passion at work.

Questions for Soul-Work

In an attempt to find or rekindle your passion within your work, ask yourself the following questions:

※ What aspects of my work do I truly love?

※ How is my work making a difference?

※ Am I using my gifts fully?

※ Who are my mentors?

※ Is the world becoming a better place because of my work?

※ What are the challenges for growth?

Questions for Soul-Death

※ What aspects of my work tire me merely by the thinking of them?

※ What original ideas have I had in the past month?

※ What percentage of my work requires no creative thinking?

※ What is my energy level while at work?

※ How many of my work mates are "nobody" to me?

※ If I were to leave tomorrow, what impact would it have?

⊠ WORK WITH PURPOSE

Why do we do the work we do? To what end is our labor being offered? Is it, in some way, work that makes a positive contribution to the world? Work is about more than productivity, or just making a living. Work is about making a positive difference for the benefit of humankind. If our life-purpose is centered around giving, is the purpose of our work consistent with the purpose of our lives? When the primary measure of our work is no longer productivity or profit, we have made a giant step toward work as art.

Many years ago, author and Roman Catholic theologian Henri Nouwen recounted his frustration whenever he was stopped by students at the university where he taught. He noted that he could hardly ever walk across campus without being interrupted by students who wanted to talk with him, and ask questions as they sought answers for their own spiritual development. He said, "All I could think of was the work I had waiting for me at my office, all the books that I needed to be writing, and that I didn't have time for these interruptions." One day, in the middle of one of these interruptions he discovered that such exchanges were not an interruption of his work, they *were* his work. Are your interruptions merely distractions? Or could they be the key to your true work?

Gerald May writes about the two forces of efficiency and love. Efficiency drives the world of business, where we need to eliminate waste, yet it is in the realm of love where we discover our passion and purpose. But efficiency at the exclusion of love creates order without heart. What would you be doing, and *love* doing, if you were not concerned about being efficient? The answer to such a question may reveal an important possibility waiting to be born.

Twentieth-century psychiatrist and author Carl Gustav Jung described life in two distinct stages. The first stage involves ego development and necessitates accumulation. It is a period of "getting." We "get" an education, a life partner, a job, a promotion, a car, or a house and all the things that fill it up, sometimes including the gift of children. It is a time of plenty during which the ego becomes satisfied with the symbols of material success.

The second stage is quite different; it is the stage of simplification and giving. This change occurs by traversing a most important event—the mid-life crisis. The Chinese character for the word "crisis" also means opportunity. Thus, the transformation from the first to the second stage of life becomes our opportunity for dramatic change.

The climax of my mid-life opportunity occurred at the age of 37, when my wife Nancy and I divorced. After an 18-year marriage, the relationship could no longer withstand the trauma of the pain that we created for one another. I separated from my family and began a long and painful period of reflection. Feeling that I was the object of the frustration as well as a disappointment to my many friends, I began to experience the true meaning of crisis and failure. If I was ever to regain inner balance as a foundation for eventual outer excellence, I had to embark upon a path of transformation and discover what had to change in my life.

I let go of the accumulations of stage one, which included my career as a parish priest and all of its trappings. I kept only my books, a clock and my desk and chair. After one year away from the West Coast, I returned to California with no job, no place to live, and $6,200 as the sum total remainder of my life's earnings. It was during this period that I began to experience fear for the first time in my life. I seemed to have very little support, and no clear direction.

Without additional financial resources coming in, yet continuing to have support expenses going out, I had to move quickly. First, however, I needed to go back to the basics and rediscover my strength and my passion, and remember the gifts I had been given.

It was during this period that I began what I eventually referred to in my first book (*Leading from the Maze*), as the "inner management practices." But I also began to discover the more authentic meaning of life-purpose. No longer interested in accumulating anything more than what was necessary to fulfill my monthly obligations, I began to ponder the question, "What is my true purpose in life?" For 20 years I had been a "professional giver." I was always "on" and was expected to heal those who were wounded and give to those in need. This was indeed my soul-work, but within a role I had relinquished and no longer desired. I knew from the still quiet voice within me that my life purpose would remain related to the action of giving. Now, however, it had to be outside the role formerly associated with that action. I would give out of choice and preference, and not because of any defined role from which giving was expected.

Anytime we serve others without expecting anything in return, we do so because giving is our reason for being. It is our soul-work, and the work that makes a difference in the lives of all who know us. It is this intention to serve that all of us, at some point in our lives, will eventually embrace. And, if we follow our passion, live our lives on purpose, use our given gifts to make a difference in the world, our very lives will become our legacy.

⊠ GIFTS FOR LEGACY

The eye that sees God is the same eye that sees me. — MEISTER ECKHART

Several years ago, during a seven-day backpack trip into Yosemite National Park, I spent two days alone, fasting, sitting and living with the challenge of being alone in the wilderness. After some time searching for the perfect spot, I pitched my tent at the base of a large tree at an elevation of 11,000 feet. Despite the imaginary bear that I was sure was trying to claw its way into my tent one night (it was a tree branch moving in the wind), I settled in for the experience of a lifetime. From my daytime perch, I could view five different valleys of Yosemite. They all seemed to have their starting point directly below me, expanding into majestic cathedrals of open space and solid granite. At night, I sat under an infinite umbrella of shooting stars, their meteoric flares searing the skies as if they were part of a search-

and-rescue mission for one of their own. It was while in this mystical place of unspeakable beauty that I fully understood that we are, indeed, made of the same material as the stars, and *we are one* with the Universe. The meteors were searching for me and the stars were the welcoming committee. I was looking for God, and God was looking for me. A connection was made.

If we can look upon the created world with an eye of such appreciation, then we can turn that same eye inward to recognize the universal beauty within ourselves. We are the product of the Creator and have the same beauty and gifts of creation within us. As the adage suggests, "The acorn does not fall far from the tree."

To publicly acknowledge our gifts is one of the most difficult tasks we face. We have been led to believe that recognition and admission are signs of arrogance; thus we shrink to a false humility and diminish our gift supply by self-deprecation. Self-knowledge includes embracing those gifts that flow through us, and then working to develop them fully.

To help people in this area of gift-recognition, I created an exercise often used in our seminars, called "The Appreciation Chair." Groups of people who have spent enough time together to get to know each other are asked to indicate what they most appreciate about one another. The person sitting in the chair can only respond to these comments with a "thank you." After the first few statements of "What I most appreciate about you is," the initial resistance naturally melts away, and a warm glow emanates from the recipient. Always very moved by this experience, the participant learns what it feels like to be recognized and appreciated by others. When we are able do this for ourselves, we can also recognize our gifts willingly.

Gift Inventory

Before beginning the following five-step inventory, look back over your life and determine what you do, or have done, well. Look for the little things that indicate talent. In my morning ritual of making coffee, I have the ability to pour water into the coffeepot exactly to the eight-cup line, without looking. Is this a gift? No. Is it a marketable quality that could provide income? Hardly. But it does suggest something about awareness and timing, both of which are critical components of my work. Such keen abilities can provide a clue as to what our gifts really are.

Values—Step One

Because values are at the core of our being, we begin here by exploring them. What we believe and what we hold sacred relate to what we value. Conflict can occur when what we value is at odds with our environment. For instance, if we value open, honest, and direct communication but are in any situation where the opposite is the norm, we will become very dissatisfied. If time-management is a low priority for us and the world of work demands it, we will encounter personal challenges to our behavior. The best relationships, whether work or personal, flourish where values are shared.

Although some values will change in accordance with the changing stages of our lives, we still have some core tenets that are forever a part of our personal fabric. For instance, honesty, integrity, family, health, and security are usually in the top-ten list. Determining what is at our core is the first step in determining our gifts.

For the purpose of tracking the five steps of the gift inventory, I will use three of my core values: freedom, relationships, and change. Freedom is at the foundation of who I am—freedom to express what I believe, live a certain lifestyle, choose relationships, create and decorate, plant, and cook. My value regarding relationships is the result of growing up in a large and close family; I honor the privilege of being a parent, and I love my family. The value of change relates to my deep desire to recreate things and make them better. It reflects my appreciation of excellence and my impatience with mediocrity. Interestingly, two of my values created conflict during my 18 years in parish ministry. Freedom for unique expression was forever limited under the scrutinizing eye of the public, while change occurred slowly, often painfully, in an institution that enjoys being a safe haven from change. With two of my three core values often in conflict with the organization's values, the one remaining value of love and relationships was not enough to keep me in this work.

As an exercise, make a list of the ten values that are most important to you at this time. Then narrow it down to the top five. Here some example of values to stimulate your thoughts:

Honesty	Integrity
Family	Friendship
Financial security	Health
Compassion	Responsibility

Personal growth	Spiritual growth
Knowledge	Power
Social action	Safety
Tradition	Self-control
Environment	Achievement

Step Two — Passion

Within each of our chosen values are passions that relate to this value. Passion, as discussed earlier, is that life-energy that surges when a value is embraced or challenged. My passion concerning freedom became very apparent recently, when I was informed that my home was on a list for potential historic status in the city where I live. Many hundreds of us are against this preservation initiative because it may give a local committee the authority to determine what we can (or cannot) change about our homes, including color and landscaping. While I am in favor of strict zoning codes, my value of freedom is threatened when I think of having my home "designed by committee."

Passion about relationships could be exhibited in building a team, beginning a romantic relationship or organizing a neighborhood as a community. Passion for change could be at the heart of developing a new physical-fitness routine, remodeling an older home, or rebuilding a broken organization. It is the same fire that runs through my veins and motivates my action. Within the context of a seminar community, my work is most rewarding when I serve as a vehicle for transformation, helping to free participants of the barriers that keep them from their most authentic selves, guiding them toward some form of lasting change. My top three values are satisfied, and that is when my work is extraordinarily fun and an art form as well.

How do we discover our passion? I like to ask the metaphorical question: "What makes my heart sing?"—when I know that, then I have found a passion source; I experience physical states such as lightness, intrigue, energy and warmth. One of my greatest passions is public speaking. Although considered the number one fear in life by the majority of humankind, I find the exhilaration of walking to a platform to begin a free form talk one of life's greatest thrills. Speaking supports my values:

⚒ Freedom—to speak without notes and be free to interact with the audience

- Relationship—connecting with an audience on the deepest level possible
- Change—speaking on subjects that "comfort the afflicted and afflict the comfortable,"

Make a list of all the ways you can passionately express your values, and narrow the list down to two items for each of your five values.

Step Three — Talents

Talents are not gifts—they are the smaller and multiple components of the larger and more singular specialty. We can have many talents that surround one gift. Review the following list of activities and check the ones that could be used to support your passionate values.

Ability to:	Advise	Instruct
	Analyze	Interpret
	Arbitrate	Lead
	Arrange	Learn
	Create Art	Listen
	Audit	Love
	Care-take	Maintain
	Classify	Manage
	Collect	Make from instructions
	Communicate	Motivate
	Compare	Negotiate
	Commit	Observe
	Compile	Organize
	Compute	Perform
	Construct	Persuade
	Coordinate	Read
	Conceptualize	Repair
	Copy, record	Research, investigate
	Demonstrate	Sell
	Design	Serve
	Display	Supervise
	Drive	Support
	Encourage	Use hands
	Evaluate	Use tools

Step Four — Gifts

The gifts we have been given are an expression of the Divine—the ultimate in creativity. They can also be genetic, flowing as easily out of us as they did from our biological parents, or they can be developed and grown like a seed through much hard work. Gifts are to be used for the benefit of many. This distinguishes them from talents. Unlike talents, a gift comes with special responsibility that surpasses unique privilege.

William Lewis is a gifted painter, yet he did not begin to follow his passion until the age of 70. Although in the art field for some years as the owner of art galleries, he never painted. Learning as much as he could from a mentor, and after twelve years of devoted effort, he now turns out beautiful paintings each day for galleries around the country. His gift is not only in the consignment of paint to canvass, but also in his ability to create art whose presence makes our dwellings richer and touches the hearts and lives of those who view it.

What gifts of yours can be used to make the lives of others richer, deeper and more whole? Here is a list for your personal assessment.

The Gifts of Leadership

Wisdom	the gift for discerning what is right, true and necessary
Vision	the gift for seeing potential and constructing a visual concept with extraordinary confidence
Management	the gift for communicating the vision and mobilizing people to work together with passion toward making the vision a reality
Administration	the gift for tending to a vision and overseeing the material resources necessary for fulfilling the vision
Serving	the gift for leading others by serving the needs of those who are led

The Gifts of Healing

Healing	the gift for serving as a channel of compassion for restoring health
Compassion	the gift for being able to immerse ourselves fully in the human condition, to genuinely feel the pain and struggles of another

Counseling	the gift for listening generously and providing words of comfort, challenge, consolation, and encouragement
Giving	the gift for contributing time and material resources freely, with joy and eagerness
Hospitality	the gift for creating an open space where trust, play, and celebration are present
Intervention	the gift for interceding in conflict with positive resolution

The Gifts of Communication

Speaking	the gift for communicating spoken words with passion, clarity, and brevity
Writing	the gift for formulating thoughts, and expressing them in writing so that they bring encouragement, guidance, knowledge, and enlightenment to the reader
Teaching	the gift for creating a learning environment in which minds are challenged and lives are improved
Music	the gift for creating or performing music for the benefit of others
Mentoring	the gift for guiding others to increase their effectiveness in the use of their own gifts
Knowledge	the gift for discovering, accumulating, analyzing, clarifying, and disseminating information
Craftsmanship	the gift for creating material objects that have lasting value

Step Five—Authentic Action

Our values, passion, purpose, and gifts often go unused without authentic action. In order to leave a lasting legacy, we must put them into service. I put my gifts for teaching, speaking, and writing into authentic action by leading seminars, giving keynote speeches, and publishing books and articles. My value of relationship guides my passion for building communities of people; my gifts of compassion, hospitality, and counseling have helped to create a neighborhood and network of remarkable people and close friends; my value for change works in tandem with my gifts for leadership and vision, to transform untapped potential into tangible form and expression. To act authentically is to "make things happen."

What action can you take that meets the needs of a hungry world? What can you do to transform mediocrity into excellence, emptiness into fullness? Ponder this and you will discover the action that will create your legacy.

Leaving a Legacy

What you leave behind is not what is engraved in stone monuments,
but what is woven into the lives of others. —PERICLES

Eight years ago, I had the opportunity to consult with a rather feisty CEO who would not budge regarding a decision clearly beneficial to his company. His entire staff agreed on the direction that needed to be taken, but it was a path directly opposed to the CEO's. I was able to see that the CEO could not perceive the wisdom in the team's position, but I needed to remain an impartial presence. Not quite sure what to do, I listened to an intuitive voice that guided me toward asking the CEO about something that he truly valued. Instead of challenging him about his position, I pulled up a chair directly in front of him and asked, "Don, what legacy would you like to leave so that when you are gone, people will remember your contribution?"

The CEO sat for a while in silence. "Well," he stammered, "this company will have provided work for many people over the years."

"Will they be better off for having worked here?" I asked.

"They will have been able to pay their bills," he replied.

"Is that enough?"

"No, I don't suppose it is."

"Then what else would you want for them?"

"I would like for them to be happy, to have enjoyed their work, and to have their lives enhanced by having been here."

The process continued until the CEO realized that his position was a barrier to achieving his ultimate desire. By reversing his position, he stopped blocking a natural process that would ultimately create a better place to work.

Better Places to Work

The science of management has traditionally fostered the belief that managers are supposed to manage people to generate high productivity for higher profit. Although I am not against productivity and profit, I believe in another concept of management—*first things first.* Good and effective management begins with managing the business of ourselves first. Knowing what baggage we bring to work and how it affects our daily behavior is the first step toward providing healthy management practices. When we are willing to take the time—and the risk—to explore who we are and how that affects the environment, we can more effectively utilize the inner management practices necessary for the work of creating individual excellence. Only then can we move to the next challenge, that of managing the environment where others work.

The CEO referred to above discovered that his legacy was having created a workplace in which authenticity, honesty, creativity and trust were valued and encouraged. In any company, where employees know that their entire self is welcome at the work-place, they can grow and thrive and, when the time is right, leave as better persons than when they joined the company. Through mentoring and guided care, employees are groomed for their next job, whether in the present company or another company.

As we grow in our ability to manage ourselves and bring forth our own authenticity, creativity and integrity, we contribute these same values to the environment in which others do their work. When the atmosphere consists of this "healthy air," we can be assured that all who work in it will bring forth the same healthy qualities that surround them.

Parents of young children learn this important lesson. The challenge is not to direct their every move and teach them their every lesson—life will present that through experience. The challenge is to create a "living room" of trust, hope, play, and love through which these most important guests of the parents' life will pass. And when they exit through the door on their way to adulthood, hopefully they will have integrated the aspects of an environment that will continue to nourish them in their own pursuit of inner balance and outer excellence.

What will be woven into the lives of others as a result of knowing us? Do we want to be remembered as those who left a legacy of light, or a testament of shadow? Will we make a difference wherever we are? Will there be more bloom to the flowers where we reside, more oxygen in the room for others wherever we take our breath, and more room to stand for those who stand next to us? Will people in our presence be encouraged to be their authentic and complete selves, able to claim their true nature without being judged?

People in life's second stage are not interested in making more money or having more power or prestige; they don't need a larger home or better car. Instead, they want only to make a difference, to do something that benefits others. They want to leave a lasting legacy that indicates life is better because they were here. Norman Cousins wrote: "If something comes to life in others because of you, then you have made an approach to immortality." Is that not the secret path to the age-old desire to live forever? The elixir of life is not found in a fountain or a magic potion, but instead is found in the emergence of life that has resulted because of you. That is immortality, and a legacy of lasting value.

The Balance Practice: Laughter

Laughter is the shortest distance between two points.
—VICTOR BORGE

Laughter is the sound that we make when we are most complete, most whole, most joyful, and most human. The word "humor" comes from the Latin word *humus,* the root of the word "human." When we laugh, we touch the deepest level of our earthiness, so when we snort, howl, sniff, bark, or whine, we are accessing our primal roots. We also tap into the center of our being—our souls. When we enjoy a good "belly laugh," the body responds by producing such healthy chemicals that disease can be abated and spirits lifted. We become energized, ready for the next challenge, ready for the next laugh. Like the flavor of a well-aged cabernet wine, each sip of laughter has its own unique quality and rich aftertaste. When we laugh together, we create relationship at an intimate level.

Former Secretary of State Henry Kissenger used a particular technique when negotiations involving international disputes became stalled. He asked the participants to table all business for one hour while everyone shared his or her favorite funny story. Although sometimes reluctant to begin, they soon experienced the fun of rich and humorous narratives. The mood of the room would change dramatically, as it became more open, playful, and receptive to new ideas. From that point, they most often moved on toward resolution.

My friend and artist, William Woodward, is one of America's finest living painters. Professor of Fine Arts at George Washington University, Bill creates art that will still be hanging in galleries centuries from now. But he is gifted with another art form almost as acute as his ability to paint: his talent for telling a humorous tale from the vast collection stored in his quick mind.

With almost any accent for any occasion, Bill is able to relate some of the funniest stories I have ever heard. He, our good friend and fellow painter Bill Lewis (another master storyteller), and I have laughed until we hurt.

Bill Woodward gets some of his material from his 13-member luncheon club in Washington, D.C., which is "dedicated to laughter." The members include such talents as comedian Mark Russell, and they gather once a month to meet the challenge of sharing a new joke or story that has never been heard before. This daunting task entails an unusual search for brief material to present in front of a most discerning audience. The gales of laughter that can be heard from behind those closed doors can only be imagined, but I have been told by Bill that it is common for the waiters to drop their trays and fall down from laughing—literally. What fun! According to the science of phoenetics, there are three kinds of sounds that we create: Dynamic Sound—the high, energetic vowel sounds of E and I; Magnetic Sound—the rounder and softer sound of O; and the Integrated Sound—"AH." It is this latter sound that the body creates when it is most satiated. We intone it at the drinking fountain when satisfying a deep thirst; at the end of a great meal when we can eat no more; and in the sound of laughter, the ultimate resonance of a creative universe.

Truth is one and the learned call it by many names.

Not surprisingly, "AH," the most complete sound, is found in every name associated with God in every world religion. In addition to more common names such as God, Jehovah, Yahweh, Messiah, Buddha, Allah, Brahman, Krishna and Shiva, there are names of divinities such as the Zoroastrian Ahura, the Sikh Guru Granth, the Jain Mahavira, the Taoist Lao Tsu, and the Shinto Kami. Likewise, names from the numerous African and South Pacific religions contain the divine sound of AH.

We can conclude that laughing is a divine act, for with each expulsion of "AH," we conjure up the sound of the Divine. Is it any wonder that we feel so much healthier when we laugh? We have done an exercise of the soul!

Laughter is a gift, and discovering the humor in many situations requires wisdom. Not everyone will allow himself or herself such enjoyment. We have all met people who would rather die than smile, as if fearful that their faces would break if even a hint of happiness were expressed. I avoid such people at all costs.

Laughter has always been one of the most significant attributes of my family. My daughters Julie and Laura have continued in the tradition of my brother and sisters. Julie's laugh is so hearty that we have been known to get up and leave our seats in a movie theater in order not to be associated with anyone "so happy." My sister Cindy will suggest that we all get together for a weekend, so "we can laugh." And laugh we do. So self-amused at our own jokes or quips that we often cannot get to the punch line without running out of breath, we will stand in a kitchen and literally "howl" about almost anything. If anyone dares to give another the lead about any subject, the repartee begins and the laughter follows.

My associate Carmela Tomasini teaches people through Jin Shin Jyutsu to "be the smile." When the body's energy rallies around this attitude, the body's face not only smiles; all cells of the body become the smile. This is natural for Carmela because she is "walking laughter." We started laughing and snorting within the first few minutes after we met, and still continue this practice 12 years later.

While visiting a cancer ward recently as a volunteer, Carmela passed out Red Vine licorice as magic wands to each of the patients, kissing and blessing each patient with her magic spell. As she brought smiles and laughter to many, she was stopped by a humorless nursing assistant who demanded to know why she was doing such a foolish thing. Undaunted by the challenge, she responded, "Those people are fighting for their lives in that room. Laughter is good and it makes the fight a little less difficult."

Carmela's "Patch Adams" type of approach is not always well-received among the "serious." Yet in many of the organization boardrooms of our world, there are people fighting for their lives. Laughter would be good for them.

Twirling

My sister Cindy grew up wearing a tutu and ballet slippers. Whenever company would visit, Cindy would appear in full costume and ask our Mother, "Can I dance and twirl for them?" She was usually granted permission. The "audience" would sit patiently while Cindy danced and twirled about the room, until her never-ending debut would be terminated by polite applause. What would a work-life be like if we were willing to bring our inner child out of hiding to twirl before each important issue? Imagine the difference in the outcome if participants got up for a "twirl break" in the midst of a difficult performance evaluation. With one spin, twirling Boards of Directors, twirling CEOs, and twirling project managers could revolutionize the way we work!

Dunt Dunt Dunt Daaa!

As children we used to announce our presence with the melodic pronouncement, "Dunt Dunt Dunt Daaa!" If you are a Baby Boomer, you may remember this tune which most likely came from some radio show that captured our imagination as we anxiously awaited the next exciting episode. Instead of firing the undeleted expletives that flow out of our mouths toward any driver who cuts us off on the expressway, we can shout out, "Dunt Dunt Dunt Daaa!" When impatient with a co-worker who has not lived up to your expectations or a boss who has frustrated your career path, shout out, "Dunt Dunt Dunt Daaa!" All else will fall into place.

Recommendations

- Try to find the humor in almost any situation
- Videotape your next meeting, watch it with your co-workers, and laugh at yourselves
- Watch funny-movie clips with others
- Have a cherry-pit spitting contest during your team meeting
- Have a marshmallow fight at your next company meeting
- Highlight each event with one funny story
- Be humorous with others without sarcasm
- Surround your workspace with your top ten favorite cartoons
- Hang everyone's baby picture on a wall
- Laugh with yourself
- Laugh until you snort
- Practice laughing when you don't feel like laughing
- "Be the Smile"
- Twirl
- Shout out, "Dunt, Dunt, Dunt, Daaa!" at every opportunity.

Weaving the Seamless Tapestry

When our work becomes the work of our soul, it is the fullest expression of the authentic self possible, and the fuel that nourishes our relationships with all those around us. We cannot have a life apart from work if we, in fact, discover our true work. The key to simultaneous living is knowing how much our work is our life. The passion, purpose and gifts that we bring to our work are the same passions, purposes, and gifts that shape the life that we share with others.

When we live with passion, our bodies are charged with a profound and enduring energy that deepens our relationships. We become more vigorous, we are more fun to be around, our eyes are ablaze, and the energy is discernible. To work with purpose is to walk our individual path, to give of the gifts we have received. And when the attitude of service guides our work, our relationships with self and others are a congruent expression of who we are and how we work. There is no difference between the person at work and the person at home.

The world around us is hungry for our authentic selves and awaits our desire to make a difference. Not only can we leave a lasting reminder that says, "I was here and made a difference;" we can also leave a legacy woven inextricably into the lives of others. Hopefully, we all will discover that our work is the work of our souls. We are a seamless fabric woven with the threads of passion and purpose and the many gifts we have been given.

Epilogue

Is This Your Life?

The bitterest tears shed over graves are for words left unsaid and deeds left undone. —HARRIET BEECHER STOWE

Imagine that a large crowd is gathering in your honor. Innumerable people who have interacted with you over your many years are arriving from everywhere that you have ever worked or lived to pay tribute to your life. As the assembly gathers, your favorite music delivers thoughtful solace for the hearts of those who mourn. Some weep, and some sit in silence, while others are ready to sing. Yet each heart that mourns the loss of your life pauses for a moment to reflect as the scheduled speakers prepare to offer their remembrances of you.

A co-worker is the first to speak. She did not always agree with you, but she offers the greatest of compliments: she respected you and she trusted you. She tells of your willingness to take a stand on difficult issues, your unwillingness to be swayed by the temptation to be popular, and your un-wavering commitment to tell the truth. She says,

"His/her courage taught me to do the things I thought I could not do, for I learned from him/her that if I do not risk anything, I risk everything. I risk losing myself." She breaks into tears as she says goodbye, and how she will miss you.

The words of others begin to flow as freely as your spirit once did.

127

Their eulogies are eloquent as they each offer their well-crafted words. But then something spontaneous happens: countless people, so moved by your contribution, stand up and share the impact you have had upon their lives. You are remembered: for your constant willingness to make time for those in your life; for focusing on what mattered and never letting the little things get in your way or bind your creativity; your celebration of life and your outrageousness and playfulness, all legendary; your making work a celebration just by your attitude; and your making a difference just by your very presence.

Your concern for the community was an expression of your connection with all of life; you never stood apart from it. While others only talked of their desire to help those in need, you were doing it. Your every contribution seemed an effortless art form, as if your excellence were almost genetic. Your laughter was always present. You left your mark as only you could do.

Yet those who knew you also knew that you struggled, and experienced fear and frustration like the rest of us. You always kept the fear and frustration in perspective, however, since they were some of your best teachers. Those present spoke of your honesty and humanness—gifts you gave to them that allowed them to be more honest and human in their own lives. Your ability to share your burdens as well as your blessings made you a teacher to many.

Your loved ones are the last to speak. They say that their relationship with you was more than the inner experience of love between two people; it was a bond that often bordered on the Divine. They speak of how you always offered options and opinions, yet never told anyone how to live. Instead, you lived life fully while others simply watched. They say they learned more from your example than your words.

The testimonials that move us to tears of gratitude and laughter are an expression of appreciation for a life that touched the hearts of so many. Those who mourn you hunger almost insatiably for more information about a life that clearly made an impact on each individual gathered there. It is evident that your legacy was substantial and the impact of your presence will remain long after these brief hours of joy have concluded. This is a testimony to one who *lived simultaneously.*

If this memorial service were yours, what would be said of you and who would be the person we would miss? What qualities and experiences would you want remembered? How many people would be better off for having known you? And who will create these memories, if not you? What legacy do you wish to leave to those who remain behind? And who will live this life and create this legacy if not you?

The world around us is hungry for our authentic selves and awaits our desire to make a positive contribution. Not only can we leave a lasting reminder that is woven inextricably into the lives of others, our work can be the legacy that says, "I was here and I made a difference." This is our purpose and the work of our souls for *we are here to discover the ways in which we can serve the common good through the gifts we have been given.* This is our final work—our lasting work—weaving the seamless fabric of passion, purpose and gifts.

Embrace it—live it—do it.

What if . . .

our lives were an art form, this gathering was an art show and we were the celebrated artists . . .

our personal care consisted of appreciating the beauty of our bodies, the delight of our minds, and the energy of an eternal spirit . . .

our relationships were a testimony to trust, honor, and reverence as we comforted those who were afflicted and afflicted those who were comfortable . . .

our work was actually the reason why we were born and the product of our passion . . .

our invitation from the Universe to enjoy life as a bountiful feast of playfulness, laughter, love and creativity was actually real and . . .

our purpose was not to accumulate material things, but to give away the gifts we had been given, making a difference in the lives of all who had the privilege of knowing us . . .

What if?

What if this is not THE END but only . . .

The Beginning!

About the Author . . .

Jeffrey Patnaude, one of the pioneers in bringing together the worlds of work and spirit, is a master teacher, speaker, author, consultant and priest. A creative and dynamic presence that evokes personal and organizational transformation, he leads 12 associates as President of the Patnaude Group, in serving corporations world wide in the area of leadership development.

As an author, Jeff clearly describes a process of self-discovery and "Inner Management" skills needed for executives and entrepreneurs who seek to enhance their behavior for more effective leadership in their business and personal lives. In *Leading from the Maze, A Personal Pathway to Leadership,* his first book, he explains, "Leadership is not what we do, but who we are," and models his belief that ". . . authentic leaders do not set out to lead others, but to lead an authentic, vital life, expressing their own lives fully."

In *Living Simultaneously, Balancing Self Care, Personal Relatiionships and Work,* he uncovers the true flow of life's events and weaves them into the tapestry of what our lives truly are; a combination of our care for others and self, relationships, and the work we do. Acknowledging these important areas of our life experience helps us to create a more meaningful and satisfying life fully expressed.

Jeff Patnaude currently resides on a farm in Northern Virginia with his family and his dog Bear.

• • •

The *Living Simultaneously Seminar,* based on the principles offered in this book, is available to groups of 15 or more. If you or your company is interested in scheduling this seminar or getting information about other programs offered, please contact The Patnaude Group, toll free 877-643-1303 on the East Coast and 800-275-5382 on the West Coast. Also, to request Jeff Patnaude as a speaker, please contact the East Coast office. Additional information may be gotten at the website—www.patnaude.com.

• • •

Books available from **White Rhino Press** written by Jeffrey Patnaude:
Leadership — *Leading from the Maze*
                 Living Simultaneously
Children's Books — *Oak & Maple* — for children experienceing divorce
             Penny — a counting book in rhyme for young children
             Witchuwit — for children dealing with the issue of death